MEDITATIONS ON MASONIC SYMBOLISM

John R. Heisner

PublishAmerica
Baltimore

First printing

At the specific preference of the author, PublishAmerica allowed this work to remain exactly as the author intended, verbatim, without editorial input.

ISBN: 1-4241-4781-6
PUBLISHED BY PUBLISHAMERICA, LLLP
www.publishamerica.com
Baltimore

Printed in the United States of America

Dedicated to the memory of my loving parents,
Bob and Elinor Heisner

Who taught me my first lessons in Freemasonry

TABLE OF CONTENTS

Introduction   9

What is a Mason?   13

Traveling in Foreign Countries   16

Beauty: The Design of God   19

The Ruffians   22

The Mystic Tie   24

An Emblem of Innocence   26

Justice in a Great Measure   29

Wisdom: The First Great Pillar   32

Chastity   34

Harmony, The Music of Masonry   36

Triune Symbolism   38

Knowledge—A Masonic Duty   40

A Point: The Beginning of all Geometrical Matter   42

Whence Came You?   44

The Principle of Brotherhood   46

In Unity 48

The Fatherhood of God 51

Humility of Mind 54

The Faithful Servant 56

A Freemason's Attitude Toward Adversity 58

History vs. Myth 60

Two Things Worth Living For 63

The Mystery of Creation 65

The Awakening 68

The Sabbath 70

Fear and Injustice 72

The First Great Light 76

Secrecy and Silence 78

So Mote It Be 81

Laborare Est Orare 83

The Square and Compasses 85

The 47th Problem of Euclid 89

The Letter "G" 92

Boaz and Jachin 94

From Darkness to Light 97

Corn, Wine and Oil 99

The Lost Word 101

The Indented Tessel 104

Freedom, Fervency and Zeal 107

Tubal-Cain 110

Freedom and Responsibility 113

The Fellowcraft 115

Within the Length of My Cable-Tow 117

A Test of Faith 120

Why are Masons Referred to as "Freemasons?" 123

The Holy Saints John 126

The Master's Hat 129

The Entered Apprentice's Apron 131

The Winding Staircase 134

Two Perpendicular Parallel Lines 136

The Cable-Tow 139

The Cornerstone 141

Network, Lily-work and Pomegranates 143

The Asherah, or Rods 146

Seven: The Sacred Number 149

The North—A Place of Darkness 151

The Trowel 154

The Widow's Sons 156

INTRODUCTION

Like Freemasonry around the world, California Freemasons promote health care, homes for the aged, education and the arts and sciences. However, the most important emphasis is placed upon promoting man's understanding of God and his relationship to the Deity. Based upon a synthesis of ancient philosophies and religions, Freemasonry has a literature and a history. The allegories it portrays reveal truths derived from that synthesis and teach that new truths are yet to be discovered. In order to promote a continuing search for knowledge, each month the members of Blackmer Lodge No. 442, Free and Accepted Masons of San Diego, California, receive a Bulletin announcing meeting dates, events, charity efforts and other news about Masons and their families. Since 2001, each monthly Bulletin has also contained an article written by Worshipful John R. Heisner, Past Master, interpreting symbols employed by Freemasonry from time immemorial to impart "wise and serious truths" about God and man's relationship to the Deity. Those articles have been edited and assembled in this work to enlighten other Freemasons and non-Masons alike about the true workings of this worldwide and ancient fraternity.

The topic for each monthly article, inspired by research, thought and prayer, sought to encourage Blackmer Masons and their families to conduct their own investigation into Freemasonry's exalted lessons about morality, virtue and public service. The articles variously explore interpretations of Masonic symbols, lessons about man's relation to the Deity, and esoteric thought.

Freemasonry is known throughout the world as an "ancient system" that once transmitted knowledge by symbols rather than the written word. That was so for the ancients, because written material was extremely limited until relatively recent times. As in times past, knowledge is also communicated through Masonic ritual, or demonstrations and dramatizations of Masonic symbols. That ritual is performed within closely guarded lodges that may only be attended by Freemasons. The ritual is secret, but the lessons taught may be studied by anyone.

The primary purpose of a Masonic lodge is to provide a forum for learning and applying instructions received in philosophy, comparative religion, liberal arts, science, grammar, rhetoric, astronomy, geometry and music. For Masons, the greatest and most sacred of these is the study of geometry.

Geometry treats of the powers and properties of magnitudes, in general, and is symbolized within by the letter "G," which is suspended in the eastern segment of a Masonic lodge room directly above the chair where the Worshipful Master sits. Of all the liberal arts and sciences, geometry is enriched with a consistency and unswerving truth about spatial relationships not found elsewhere in other disciplines. That fact is intended to inspire Masons, as well as all mankind to reflect upon the consistency and unswerving truth of the Deity and to learn how and why His laws are so similar to the unalterable theorems of geometry. Freemasonry looks to the study of geometry as an analogy to the more important task of living a life that rests upon the spiritual fundamentals of faith, hope and charity.

A Freemason is a man of the age of 18, or older, who professes a belief in one Supreme Being, and who has been voluntarily initiated into Freemasonry through a solemn symbolic ceremony performed by members in good standing of a Masonic Lodge. The candidate for Freemasonry proceeds in his Masonic journey first as an Entered Apprentice exploring and absorbing the basic fundamentals taught by Freemasonry. Next, the candidate advances to the second degree as a Fellowcraft and commits himself to acquiring a broader understanding of the liberal arts and sciences. Finally, upon advancing to the third or sublime degree of Master Mason, the candidate is exposed to the valuable lessons of mortality and immortality and investigates the reality of his own soul. During his journey, the candidate for Masonic degrees also openly professes several vows of fidelity and honor, the specifics of which relate exclusively to Freemasonry and are therefore never revealed to non-Masons. The candidate further commits himself to serving the Deity and His laws; promoting the welfare of all Masons, their widows and orphans; and working to make the world where he lives a better place.

The Masons of Blackmer Lodge No. 442 are members of one the oldest Masonic Lodges in San Diego. Its Charter was issued by the California Grand Lodge on October 15, 1914. "Like the history of a nation, the history of Blackmer Lodge No. 442 is comprised of the record of the character and achievements of the men who compose it," wrote Blackmer Past Master, Warren Libby. Indeed, Blackmer Masons are deeply indebted to Worshipful Libby for preserving a record of the early history of that distinguished lodge and the accomplishments of the various members.

The Lodge was named by a vote of the original Charter Members in honor of Eli Tucker Blackmer, Past Master of San Diego Lodge No. 35. Worshipful Blackmer was a prominent educator, concert director, civic leader, Masonic leader and former Colonel in the U.S. Army.

From its inception, Blackmer Lodge grew rapidly. At the end of the first year of its existence, the Lodge boasted of 80 Charter Members representing 31 different occupations and walks of life. Membership climbed to 174 by the end of World War I, reached 840 at the close of World War II, and stood at 1,295 in 1954. In that year, Blackmer Lodge was easily one of the largest Masonic Lodges not only in California, but the entire United States of America. To this day, it continues to enjoy a statewide reputation for performing excellent Masonic ritual in the form and manner officially approved by the California Grand Lodge. Its present day members are from diverse religious and social backgrounds, represent numerous professions, trades and industries and continue to promote Masonic education and charitable works. The Lodge has maintained a high "honor roll" status in its support of California Masonic Homes and service to the widows of deceased Blackmer Masons.

Representative of the diverse nature of Blackmer Masons, the author of this work, John R. Heisner, has been a Master Mason for 38 years and is the descendant of several Freemasons. His great-grandfather was Master Mason, the Grand Secretary of the Nebraska Grand Lodge, a Knights Templar, a York Rite Mason and a Past Master of his Nebraska Masonic Blue Lodge. His maternal grandfather was a Master Mason, Scottish Rite Mason and Shriner. His father was a Past Master of a California Masonic Blue Lodge, a 50 year member of California Freemasonry and the Scottish Rite, as well as a Charter Member of Tehran Shrine Temple. His mother is a Past Matron of the Order of Eastern Star, who was renowned for her excellence in delivering ritual. His brother is a former member of DeMolay.

Worshipful Heisner is a Past Master of Blackmer Lodge, a 32nd degree Scottish Rite Mason, York Rite Mason, Knights Templar and Shriner. He is also a Committeeman for the California Grand Lodge, a member of the Allied Masonic Degrees, the Knights of the Red Cross of Constantine and the College of Rosicrucians. In addition to this literary work in Freemasonry, Worshipful Heisner leads a committee in the San Diego Scottish Rite that researches, writes and speaks about the 32 degrees of Scottish Rite Masonry to other Scottish Rite Masons.

Since 1973, Worshipful Heisner has also practiced law in the State of California and is admitted to all courts of record in that state, as well as numerous federal districts. He served as a prosecutor for approximately 12 years and has been in private practice since 1986. Presently a shareholder in the San Diego law firm of Sullivan Hill Lewin Rez & Engel, Worshipful Heisner has also taught a trial advocacy class at the University of San Diego Law School for approximately 12 years.

WHAT IS A MASON?

"Thou shalt have no other gods before me."
Ex. 20:3

Numerous articles have been written in various Masonic periodicals describing, discussing and examining a host of characteristics and personal attributes common among Freemasons. At the head of the list is usually the fact that Freemasonry is a "fraternity" that assists its members to improve themselves as trustworthy citizens; to responsibly participate in the communities in which they live; and devotedly serve educational foundations, charitable enterprises and free health services sponsored, managed and operated by Masons. However, few focus squarely upon that which truly sets Freemasonry apart from other worthwhile community service organizations.

Indeed, Freemasonry cares for the poor; sponsors educational scholarships; supports and maintains hospitals, clinics and residential facilities for senior citizens and the disadvantaged; and even offers free eye transplants, surgeries and general care to members and their families. Yet, the same is true of several other organizations that share in a like-minded manner Freemasonry's dedication to giving. Those endeavors are not only worthwhile, they are essential to the quality of life we most desire to perpetuate in our great Nation. Nevertheless, they do not uniquely distinguish Masons from others. That "uniqueness" may be found in the manner each Mason approaches and shapes his personal relationship with the Deity.

Masonry does not teach men to believe in one God, to behave according to a specific moral code, or to engage in acts of loving kindness we call "charity." A candidate for the degrees of Freemasonry is expected to bring those beliefs with him when he joins the fraternity, where he will find them encouraged and reinforced. Any candidate who expects Freemasonry to teach him the true path to God will soon realize his error. Masonry leaves those matters to the Rabbis, the Priests, the Ministers and the Imams.

History has taught the world that arguments about religious differences among men can wrench apart the harmonious fabric of society and plunge whole nations into violence, death and despair. Consequently, Freemasonry itself is not a religion and refuses to promote any one religion to the exclusion of others. Rather, Masons believe firmly in each man's freedom to choose the religion most suited to him—a freedom that is regarded so reverently that it is among those cited in the First Amendment to the United States Constitution. It is this belief that truly distinguishes Freemasonry and the members who are called "Masons."

A study of the American Revolutionary War and of the times preceding it reveals that even our original thirteen colonies had a difficult time with the concept of freedom of religion. In fact, each colony had its own state-sponsored religion with the right to tax citizens for the support of each respective religious denomination. That state of affairs mirrored the reality around the globe: nations everywhere sported state-sponsored religions and often criminalized deviations from the practice of that religion. Since there was then no model anywhere on the face of the Earth from which our Founding Fathers could learn the importance of "freedom of religion," one must look to the institution of Masonry itself and discover exactly how that concept became a cornerstone of our Nation's First Amendment.

During the era of 1776, only Freemasons espoused the idea that men be free to pursue whatever religion they chose. A study of the people central to forging our country's Declaration of Independence, Bill of Rights and Constitution discloses that many held membership in Freemasonry in common regardless of their varied and respective views about church and religion. That fact is the very reason that from the outset of its existence, our Nation's laws have provided the widest latitude among society for the worship of God.

History also teaches us that Masons have regularly labored in the protection of that freedom, while many religions have labored to perpetuate their institutions to the exclusion of others. Freemasonry does not sponsor any particular religion, while many religions persist in attempting to convince "non-believers" of their error. Yet, Masons are not irreligious. Freemasonry encourages each individual Mason to attend, serve and support the church and religion of his choice. Ironically, Freemasonry has far too often been condemned and falsely persecuted by some for promoting such free choice. Indeed, throughout history certain segments of society have violently attacked Masons as being heretical simply because Freemasonry as an institution does not and never will endorse any specific religious dogma to the exclusion of all others.

As a fraternity, we should fondly think about our Masonic predecessors who taught each of us that no man's particular "error," i.e., view of God and theology, should be preferred over the "error" of another.

The next time you are asked, "What is a Mason?" instead of offering the stock reply, "a member of a fraternal society dedicated to self-improvement and charitable works," remember that your Craft's greatest contribution to the formation of this country was the expression of the belief in one Supreme Being, who desires that each man inherit His blessings, and who asks that each person respond to His call freely, deliberately, and uniquely.

TRAVELING IN
FOREIGN COUNTRIES

"For we know that if our earthly house of this
tabernacle were dissolved, we have a
building of God, an house not
made with hands, eternal
in the Heavens."
2Cor.5:1

Masonry is a succession of allegories, the mere vehicles for great lessons in morality. It speaks in symbols and sheds light upon "secrets" no living person can fully discern—future life after death. Ancient Craft Masonry provides the necessary "working tools" for use in our daily lives; "working tools" that can prepare us to eventually welcome death, not as a grim tyrant, but as a kind messenger sent to translate us from this imperfect world to that all perfect celestial Lodge above where the Supreme Architect of the Universe forever presides.

The ritual performed during the sublime degree of Master Mason explains to the candidate that the lessons taught him are intended to enable him to "obtain wages while traveling in foreign countries." Masonic writers have frequently interpreted this symbolism to mean that while living on this Earth, we are to conduct our lives as men of character, integrity and piety. Yet, while that interpretation is certainly substantial, it is incomplete.

Consider this passage from sacred scripture: "Man that is born of woman is of few days and full of trouble. He cometh forth like a flower and is cut down. He fleeth, also, as a shadow and continueth not." In other words, our earthly existence has a beginning and an ending. It consists of a wonderful journey through this world, this material plane, this identifiable land from the day of our birth to the time of our demise. As Master Masons, we are further instructed upon the truth that our death does not result in annihilation. Indeed, we are "translated" into a new and different existence—a "foreign country"—where the soul of man will continue a journey that we can neither presently know, nor fully understand.

It is while traveling in that realm that Masons anticipate receiving "wages:" that celestial land "from whose bourn no traveler returns." Thus the term "foreign country" has a profound spiritual meaning to weighed and considered as seriously as we weigh and consider the lessons of morality applied to our earthly existence. From the square and compasses, we are reminded of the truth: "as it is above, so shall it be below." The lessons learned lead Masons to conclude that the morality we learn to live here below will, if lived well, entitle us to "wages," or reward when we travel above.

In Blue Lodge Masonry, the lessons derived from the various symbols teach us what the Ancients instructed the elite: when physical life ends, man is resurrected to a new and different existence. Masons are inspired to make this life a credit to the future by extending charity, or love to all mankind, regardless of race, religion, creed or doctrine. As spiritual beings, we should also anticipate the fullness of new life as the just reward, or "wages," of our faithfulness. That fullness is expected by Masons to the brightest light emanating from the presence of God when we are once again figuratively asked, "being in a condition of darkness, what do you most desire?"

Although Freemasonry is not a religion and has never been promoted as a substitute for religion, it does offer a road map for the religious man to follow. From sacred scripture we learn that, "(P)ure religion and undefiled before God is this: to visit the orphans and widows in their time of affliction and to keep ourselves spotless before the world." (Jas.1:27). This passage represents the very foundation of Masonic charity. When we practice such Masonic charity we may be assured that once the Supreme Architect finally brings us from darkness to that eternal light, we will be deemed faithful and worthy of the "wages" He will provide us while "traveling in that foreign country."

BEAUTY:
THE DESIGN OF GOD

"For the Lord taketh pleasure in His people:
He will beautify the meek with salvation."
Ps. 149:4

Operative Freemasonry's chief objective in architecture was to accomplish beauty and symmetry, as was accomplished in the building of King Solomon's Temple. Speculative Masonry emphasizes the beauty of character and the virtues of true manhood. Symbolically, "beauty" is one of three principle supports of a Masonic Lodge. It is represented by the Corinthian column, the most beautiful of the ancient orders of architecture, as well as by the Junior Warden, who symbolizes the meridian sun—the most beautiful object in the heavens. Fellowcraft Masons are instructed during the second degree of Freemasonry that five original orders of architecture were studied by Freemasons. The Corinthian, created by the Greeks, was considered the more beautiful of all of the orders. Hiram Abif, who Masonic tradition informs us was the the Grand Master in charge of the building of King Solomon's Temple, is for that reason also represented by the column of beauty.

Lessons in Freemasonry teach us that as a symbol, "beauty" is intended to inspire us to study and attain a deeper understanding about the dignity of human nature, as well as about the vast powers and capacities of the human soul. Our attention is invited to the literary works of all great writers, including Plato and Aristotle, not merely those whom we refer to as "Masonic authors," such as Albert Pike and A. E. Waite. Although man is encompassed within a dome of incomprehensible wonders, he is given an array of freedoms and choices. He is certainly more than a mere object upon which God's light is to fall. Rather, as human beings we respond to that which stimulates us to action—the good as well as the evil. On the one hand, the response can be a loathing of mankind in general, or merely of certain specific people because of true or imagined infractions. Whole nations and religious bodies have ventured into violent and deadly conquests simply because those upon whom horror was inflicted thought, behaved and believed differently. On the other hand, the more beautiful response, the response Freemasonry encourages, recognizes that although man is faulty by nature, we are all conducted by the same divine radiance emanating from the Great Architect of the Universe. God's light shines upon everyone; the good as well as the evil.

All of the ancient religions recognized a tension between light and darkness; good and evil; order and disorder. The Deity, universe and human intellect may best be understood as a complete and harmonious organism. Mankind is called to assume its role within that organism that while we are unique individuals, we are all proceeding through life with our own share of pain, sorrow, illness and suffering. To Masons, it matters not that we suffer, it matters how we handle our suffering.

Like the beauty of a developing human soul, beauty in architecture is distinctive. Who can legitimately challenge the majesty of the spires atop the churches situated throughout Europe where the Operative Masons labored so extensively? And, who can question the distinctiveness of a human soul that seeks to attain wisdom and knowledge for the purposes of serving his fellows, his country and his God?

Within the confines of each man's suffering, the soul truly yearns to shout, "Thank you, Father of All Creation, for finding me worthy to be tested." And once tested, to be found worthy in spite of our personal sorrows and needs to teach and share wisdom with others; in short, to serve mankind to God's glory. Indeed, my brother, that is the "beauty and glory of the day"—and the noblest work of man.

THE RUFFIANS

"And ye shall know the truth, and
the truth shall make you free."
John 8:32

At the heart of the mysteries of Freemasonry lies a legend from which one learns how three unworthy craftsmen working at the Temple of Solomon entered into a plot to extort from a famous Freemason a secret they had no right to know. No man can sit in witness of that pertinent ritual without sensing that there is, indeed, a secret which each Master Mason has not yet won the right to know from the Great Architect of the Universe. That secret relates to how, when and in what manner good will be victorious over evil.

To those who trace Masonic symbolism to ancient Sun worship, the three Ruffians, or unworthy craftsmen, are the three winter months in the year that plot to murder the beauty and glory of summer. To those who find the origins of Freemasonry to lie in the Ancient Egyptian Mysteries, the legend is a drama about Typhon, the spirit of evil, who slays Osiris, the spirit of good, and who to Typhon's dismay is ultimately and triumphantly resurrected to life. Others will find a connection between the legend to the life and death of Jesus, who was put to death outside the city gate by three of the most ruthless "Ruffians" known to man—the Priest, the Politician, and the Mob. Some may identify the Ruffians, or assassins as the three renegade knights, who falsely accused the Knights Templar and thereby aided King Philip of France and Pope Clement to abolish

Templarism and slay its Grand Master.

Albert Pike, that giant of Masonic philosophy, identified the three Ruffians as the greatest enemies of individual welfare and social progress ever to exist: kingcraft, priestcraft and the ignorant mob-mind. The first enemy strikes a blow at the throat, the seat of freedom of speech. The second enemy stabs at the heart, the home of freedom of conscience. And, the third enemy fells its victim dead with a blow to the brain, which is the throne of freedom of thought.

Of the three Ruffians, perhaps the most terrible, ruthless and brutal is the ignorant mob-mind. It is so easily inflamed, so hard to restrain and so willing to wreak havoc where peace once prevailed. No tyrant or wicked priest can reduce a nation to slavery until it is first lost in the darkness of ignorance—the fruit of the mob-mind. Pike concluded that when the Ruffians murdered the Great Mason, they symbolically robbed not only their fellow craftsmen, but also themselves of the most precious secret of personal and social life—the knowledge to not only understand right from wrong, but to do good rather than evil. Pike believed that to be so because he knew that what men are together is determined by what each is alone.

One cannot get to the heart of real truth until it is admitted that there is within man himself a certain moral perversity; a spirit of mischief, which does wrong deliberately and in direct contravention to that which is known to be right. Here, truly is the real Ruffian most to be feared—the one who can be overcome only by self-discipline, the practice of that which is virtuous, and prayer for Divine assistance. It is that Ruffian of the dark, lurking in our own minds and hearts, who leads us to hurt rather than help a brother, who lays us up in idle inactivity when duty calls, and who must be taken without the gates of the city and executed from our very minds. We dare not appease him, turn a blind eye to his mischief, or tolerate his presence in our innermost being. Otherwise we, too, shall be felled dead at his feet.

THE MYSTIC TIE

"Behold, how good and how pleasant it is
for brethren to dwell together in unity!"
Ps. 133:1

Many symbols, as well as the several tenets of Freemasonry that
they represent, are termed "mystical," because they are known and
understood best by those men who have received the rites of the
Order. In a similar sense, the term "mystic tie" refers to the sacred
and inviolable bond that unites Masonic brethren. This tie stems
from the vows of eternal brotherhood made by each Mason,
irrespective of differences in religion, race, or nationality. Men of the
most discordant opinions in worldly matters are united into one
fellowship, meet at one altar, combine their energies to work charity
and are thus called "Brethren of the Mystic Tie."

Freemasons are reminded of that mystic tie during the conferral of
the Entered Apprentice Degree, as the candidate for initiation is
conducted once around the lodge room to demonstrate to the
Worshipful Master and brethren that he is duly and truly prepared for
inclusion into membership. As the initiate takes his vows and the
cable tow is removed, the brethren are also reminded that the
physical ties among people are less significant than the spiritual
bonds of loyalty and fraternal affection. Those spiritual ties are
emblematic of the tenderness with which the Supreme Architect of
the Universe embraces all of His children with the affluence of His
love. Care and concern for a brother in Freemasonry, then, inclines

the spirit of man to a sense of caring for God.

The mystic tie in Freemasonry, unlike the symbolic silver chord referred to in the Old Testament of the Holy Bible, which is severed upon man's death, once forged is never broken—it is truly eternal. As a reminder of that truth, Freemasons celebrate a ritualistic memorial for a departed brother uniting themselves with that brother's passing to the Celestial Lodge above.

Freemasons are also reminded of their strong ties of brotherhood when they read and absorb Masonic writings, learn about the good deeds performed by past great Masons and marvel at the numerous institutional charities established by Freemasons long before the living were born. Indeed, the very practice of Masonic ritual reminds every Freemason that mankind is destined to participate in the greatest mystery of all—the gift of eternal life. When it is understood that all men are so destined, it becomes easier to also understand that it is incumbent upon us to accept men as God has made them, the world as He has made it, and make the best we can of all.

AN EMBLEM OF INNOCENCE

"Your lamb shall be without blemish…"
Ex. 12:5

Masonic tradition informs us that in all ages the lamb has been deemed an emblem of innocence. Hence, it is required that a Mason's Apron should be made from lambskin to symbolize the innocence a Freemason is to retain and exercise throughout his lifetime. In the higher degrees of Freemasonry, as well as in the chivalric degrees, the lamb serves as a symbol of the biblical Paschal Lamb of the Jewish Passover, which is also a symbolical archetype of Jesus, who is regarded as the Christ by our Christian brethren—the spiritual "Lamb of God."

Freemasons are required to strive after perfect innocence in all life's relations, especially in Masonic relationships. The pure white lambskin apron worn by Masons during all Masonic approved assemblies is intended to constantly remind us of that very requirement and duty. That apron constitutes the first gift bestowed upon a candidate for degrees in Freemasonry. It also represents a Mason's responsibilities.

In ancient Israel, the apron, or "girdle," formed a part of the vestment of the priesthood—known in Gnostic circles as the Vestments of Zadok. Like a Freemason's apron, those aprons were also white and made from lambskin. White denoted purity and the lambskin denoted innocence. While Masonic ritual teaches a connection with operative class Masons, who variously wore aprons to protect their clothing from being soiled, the lambskin's significance as a priestly garment cannot be overlooked. It is from that priestly connection that a Mason's responsibilities toward mankind flow.

Like the Ten Commandments given by God to Moses, Freemasonry also has another Decalogue, which constitutes both a Masonic law to initiates, as well as a Masonic definition of the phrase "purity and innocence:" (1) God is eternal, of supreme intelligence and inexhaustible love, and is therefore to be revered and honored by the practice of the four cardinal virtues, temperance, fortitude, prudence and justice; (2) a Freemason's soul, like the souls of all mankind, is immortal—he is not to do any act that would degrade it; (3) Freemasons are to war against vice unceasingly, submit to the light of wisdom and knowledge, and do unto others that which we would have them do unto us; (4) Freemasons are to pay respect and do homage to the aged, instruct the young, and protect and defend infancy; (5) a Mason should cherish his wife and children, love his country and obey it's laws; (6) as a Freemason, the man you call a friend shall become a second self; (7) Freemasons are to avoid and flee from insincere relationships; (8) Masons are not permitted to allow any passion to become his master; (9) a Mason should hear much, speak little, and act well; and, (10) Freemasons are to study to know men, to learn about themselves, to be just, and to avoid idleness. The most important lesson learned from this Decalogue is to love one another, for its is also written in the sacred writings, as well as in the hearts of every Mason that he who claims to live in the light, yet hates his brother, is still in darkness. The Freemason will understand when such a man is also described as continuing to wear his "hoodwink."

Brethren, do not believe that you can affect nothing; do not despair; and, above all else, do not become inert. Many great deeds are accomplished from the small struggles in life. Misfortune, isolation, abandonment, and poverty are life's battles whose heroes are those who work each day to lessen their sad effects upon man and society. The lambskin, then, reminds each Freemason to become a priest, a soldier, a brother and a friend—pray with an innocent heart, war against vice with a pure conscience, and embrace a brother and friend with inexhaustible love.

JUSTICE IN A GREAT MEASURE

"To do justice and judgment is more acceptable
to the Lord than sacrifice."
Prov. 21:3

The lessons of the Entered Apprentice degree teach us to act uprightly in our dealings with all mankind, and to never fail to act justly toward ourselves, our brethren, or the world. Justice, then, is the cornerstone upon which we are instructed to erect our Masonic superstructure. For, justice in a great measure constitutes the cement of civil society. Without it, universal confusion would reign, lawless force could replace equity, and social intercourse might no longer occur.

Through His wisdom, God has given to each of us the opportunity to follow His plan for just relationships. A Freemason need look no farther than the Ten Commandments how we may participate in His plan. If tempted to steal what belongs to another, we are to resist. If we give in to the temptation, we are to repay what was taken, make amends with our neighbor and sin no more. Man is tempted by many similar passions arising from lust, greed and vanity. Freemasons are taught that it is not only forbidden to grant control of oneself to one's passions, it is unjust.

To the law of God, Freemasonry adds an imperative contract obligation upon every Mason. Upon entering the Order, or fraternity,

29

the initiate binds himself by a solemn vow to every other Mason in the world. The initiate becomes a brother to others he does not and may never know. He becomes responsible to families he may never see. He promises to aid widows and orphans who are not yet widows, or orphans. In essence, he becomes obligated to people other than himself to whom he owes duties of kindness, sympathy and compassion.

In return for his vows, the initiate becomes entitled to call upon every other Mason in the world for assistance when in need, protection when in danger, sympathy when in sorrow, attention when ill, and a burial when dead. These constitute reciprocal responsibilities of the fraternity to the initiate and are emblematic of the just dues to be given, as a standard or boundary of right, to every man by every Mason.

While performing his just duties, a Freemason is uniquely guided by principles of impartiality to act toward other men, women and children without regard to their race, religion, creed, or political beliefs. It is not for error in such beliefs or walks of life for which we chastise our brother (they are his beliefs and as such are his to hold), but for his intolerance of others and when he lacks charity toward all mankind.

Freemasons do not accuse fellow brethren for exercising a different philosophy. Rather, a lack of kindness to others is accused, as is a lack of sympathy, or a lack of integrity. Freemasons do not love their brethren because they think alike. Rather, brethren are loved simply because they are brethren. And, Freemasons do not return an unkind act with yet another—they restore troubled souls with compassion

Within the world itself, Freemasons are also expected to treat all human beings as brothers; especially those who are hateful, spiteful and wish everyone ill. Societies establish laws to guide the people who live within them. God establishes laws for all to follow, regardless of the society within which one lives. So, too, does Freemasonry extend it's "laws," or rather it's harmonious tenets, that every Mason may know that he is as much "at labor" outside of his lodge as he is when he is inside.

As Freemasons, we are also taught to regard the laws of the land in which we respectively live as deserving of our complete and unhesitating devotion. Thus, it is not for the Freemason to pick and choose which laws to follow, but to follow all of them and make equal application of them all. Masons are expected to act for the preservation of freedoms whether in the form of public education, or the selection of houses of worship, and to judge each other by the extent of charity freely given. When given in a great measure, the good it serves is limitless. The old are comforted, the ill healed, orphans have fathers, widows are not alone, and God's justice is meted out to every man, woman and child.

WISDOM: THE FIRST GREAT PILLAR OF MASONRY

"If any of you lack wisdom, let him ask God,
that giveth to man liberally, and upbraideth not;
and it shall be given him."
Jas. 1:5

In Ancient Craft Masonry, wisdom is symbolized by the "East," the place of light, which is also represented in a lodge by a pillar that stands in the east as the great support of a lodge—the Worshipful Master. Wisdom is also represented in Masonic tradition by King Solomon, who prayed to God that above all things in His power to give, he most desired the wisdom God could provide. Therefore, wisdom is recognized in Freemasonry as divine power—the creative energy of Deity. In short, wisdom seeks, by observation, experience and reflection to know things in their essence.

The lessons in Freemasonry teach us that it is necessary for a man to learn wisdom so that he may contrive, in other words to create. Above all else, Masonry invites each of us to consider the dignity of human nature and to ponder the vast powers and capacities of the human soul. The opposites in the world challenge each of us, not to fathom why they exists as much as to support the one and defeat the other. Good health is promoted by Masonic hospitals while illness is chased away. Joy is brought into the life of an isolated widow who is honored at a luncheon, eliminating, even if only for an hour or two, the ravages of sorrow. Brethren rejoice in the success of each other and lend a listening ear when one brother is overwhelmed by failure and disappointment. Life is promoted while death is put in its place as nothing more than a translating event.

One seems never to know the true meaning what it is he or she has until it is lost. Too frequently, people fail to appreciate the wealth of meaning found in the fond sayings of a parent, a child, or a friend, until that parent, child, or friend is no longer alive. Yet, to the truly wise person, nothing that is sincerely loved is ever lost. Instead of counting absence as loss, the truly wise meditates upon the memories, using the mind to resuscitate the dead and to animate visions of the past.

True wisdom recognizes the fleeting nature of our earthly existence. Humans are mortal, but there is a spiritual part that never dies. Our lives are lived here on earth as we choose while eternity yawns before us. Amidst the unseen presence of our ever loving God, each man's mind gives him the character by which he may judge how well he has lived and how worthy he is of eternal life. If he is truthful to himself, the wise man knows he is unworthy, but that God's love has endured transforming him from a person in the dark to a luminous individual who lives in the light.

The wise man despises selfishness, apathy, indifference and inaction. It is these that make men and Freemasonry ineffectual, as if like the pyramids they were doting with age and had forgotten the memory of the best traits most admired in those who have before us.

To better embrace wisdom, a Freemason can seek to revive within himself those faded impressions of generosity and self sacrifice. No man can suffer and be patient, struggle and conquer, improve and be happy without first having hope and a complete reliance upon the beneficence of God. His beneficence teaches us that extending joy to others is the just return of the grace given to us. The wise man learns how to act toward others by clearly observing and imitating how the Great Creator acts toward him and all creation.

CHASTITY

"Neither shalt thou desire thy neighbor's wife,
neither shalt thou covet thy neighbor's house, his
field,…or anything that is thy neighbor's."
Deut. 5:21

From time immemorial, one of the chief characteristics of Freemasonry has been its uncompromising demand for adherence by its members with the seventh and tenth Commandments as a matter of promoting personal purity. In a peculiar devotion, Freemasonry stands for the protection of the *chastity* of womanhood, as every Mason knows by virtue of the sacred vows he has assumed. The deeper meaning of those vows relates to the obligation it imposes upon each individual Mason to himself remain chaste.

This sacred vow requires putting into daily practice a life completely devoid of covetousness and indifference. Succinctly stated, living a chaste life means living in conformity with the spiritual law. When a person does so, he or she is regarded as being *chaste*. It is entirely irrelevant whether that man or woman is married or celibate.

Contrary to popular belief, the practice of chastity that is imposed upon Masons is not solely related to matters of sex. Rather, it bears equally on all other domains wherein there is a choice between light and darkness, good and evil. For example, fanaticism is a sin against chastity, because a fanatic is carried along in his or her path by a dark and violent current. The French Revolution, initiated on ground of justice, became an orgy of perverse collective intoxication, as did the revolution in Russia. Nationalism, whether rearing its head in Nazi Germany, or elsewhere around the globe, is similarly a form of collective intoxication drowning the conscience of the heart. Therefore, it is wholly incompatible with the state of chastity.

When a candidate for degrees in Freemasonry is brought from darkness to see the light by which Masons work, he is immediately introduced to the characteristic of chastity. The square and compasses remind us to circumscribe our desires and keep our passions within due bounds toward all mankind. That obligation also requires that a Mason avoid ever participating in the collective intoxication of fanaticism, to obey the laws of the country in which he resides and to conduct his affairs with all mankind in a just manner.

One can easily miss the significant point of chastity, if one fails to see that it is a part of the characteristic of charitableness. Along the Masonic journey, each Mason is taught to regard his fellow brother as another self—a human being who should be treated with the same care and affection that one dotes upon himself. When a Mason, or any other person does so, he or she is exercising chastity, in that he or she is acting in conformity with the spiritual law of doing unto others that which you would have them do unto you. Chastity, then, may be regarded as that state of being in which man is content with what God has given him, and being content, he is made whole.

HARMONY:
THE MUSIC OF MASONRY

"I will sing of the mercies of the Lord forever:
with my mouth will I make known thy
faithfulness to all generations."
Ps. 89

Freemasonry's archetypal definition of harmony—beauty, symmetry and order in matter and spirit—is best demonstrated by the rich and consistent application of beauty, symmetry and order in the world of music. Of all things to which we are daily exposed, bad music, unappealing music, or noisy music can rankle our nerves quicker than can an unkind remark by another person. Some people avoid attempting to play a musical instrument, or to sing a song, because they do not want to create an ugly sound. But, in the hands of a skilled musician, an instrument can be nearly brought to life filling the concert hall with the most melodious beauty, the most perfect symmetry and the most structured order that is referred to as harmony.

There exists a true relationship between Freemasonry and music. One published author has devoted an entire tome to that study, which he aptly entitled, "The Harmony of Spheres." The concept of planets and stars harmoniously filling the cosmos is like the harmonious mingling of tones which produce to the most vivid imagination an overwhelming sense of well being. Philosophers, astronomers and mathematicians have been duly inspired over the years by melodious musical harmonies, which in turn have provided mankind with a rich poetry and literature upon which men have meditated from times of antiquity to the present day.

Astronomy and harmonics, which is concerned with the movement of sounds, each employ arithmetic and geometry to measure the quality and quantity of principle movements. It is within both of those disciplines that one may discover Freemasonry's unique relationship to music, revealed in the writings of such Masonic patrons as Ptolemy and Pythagoras. Ptolemy proved heliocentricity by mathematics, while Pythagoras may have been the founder of music when he applied harmonics to geometric progressions to prove that all sound was based upon mathematics.

Everything that is governed by natural law partakes of some rational order with regard to its movement. Expanding upon his notions of a sun centered universe, Ptolemy applied mutually consistent disciplines of spatial symmetry to musical harmony and concluded in a posthumously published work that the movement of sound, like the movement of stars, is governed by certain harmonic relationships. Pythagoras applied his exceeding knowledge of mathematics to a study of conjunct tetra chords and octave ratios, reasoning that there is a special relationship between Freemasonry's sacred numbers 3, 5 and 7, and tonal consonance. That is, the numbers 3, 5 and 7 are essential to harmonious music. When those numbers are not present, the sound produced is ugly, chaotic and unstructured. Both Ptolemy and Pythagoras respectively inferred from their studies that harmonious music has a beneficial impact upon the human soul.

Masonic orders routinely employ music during their ceremonies. The connection to Freemasonry's rich mythical past is made plain: men with Masonic educations have applied the lessons of Freemasonry to discover that the harmonious intersection of melodious sound with splendid doctrine creates a harmonic power that feeds the soul with thoughts of loving kindness. Consequently, in order that a Mason might completely enjoy and understand the lessons offered in degree ritual, it is strongly recommended that each ceremony be accompanied by the playing of harmonious melodies.

TRIUNE SYMBOLISM

"Therefore speak I to them in parables: because they
seeing see not; and hearing not neither do
they understand."
Matt. 13:13

Many of Freemasonry's most sublime truths are conveyed to us in
veiled allegories and are made visible to us by the accompanying
ancient symbols. The greatest of these, the "Lost Word," is
concealed within various groups of three symbols, each group
building upon the other to teach us the Masonic meaning of the word
"trinity." Each group may be considered as a vehicle of information
necessary to aid in the comprehensive struggle to learn about God,
nature, the government of the universe and about the existence of
sorrow and evil. After careful study and reflection, one may more
specifically understand the "principle of First Cause" of all things—
that which is often referred to as the "absolute," or "Word."

See, hear, and understand what Freemasonry says about trinity.
Three pillars figuratively support a lodge: wisdom, strength and
beauty. The Egyptians and Hebrews based their respective civil
policies upon the wisdom of selected priests, the power and strength
of civil chiefs, and the resulting harmonious prosperity of the State.
The duration, or term of Masonic apprenticeship was three years,
because the Ancient Mysteries required three years' preparation by
a candidate before he could be initiated. The alarm at the door of a
lodge is given by three raps. There are three moveable and three

immoveable jewels; three principle officers in a lodge, three great and three lesser lights; three journeys by the candidate around the lodge; three questions put to the candidate prior to his admission into a lodge; three letters in the tetragrammaton of the Hebrews, or ineffable Word; and three syllables in the substitute for the "Lost Master's Word," which could be communicated only when King Solomon, Hiram, King of Tyre and Hiram Abif were all present.

In a more material fashion, the number three also represents unity and each group of veiled allegories demonstrates how the number three actually "forms one:" one lodge; one body of brethren; one "Word;" and, one God. Freemasonry teaches three theological virtues: faith, hope and charity—neither of which exists apart from the other two in the conduct of a Mason while fulfilling his duty to God, his country, and his neighbor.

Blue Lodge Freemasonry offers three degrees to worthy candidates, neither one of which can make a complete Mason without the other two. Those three degrees of Masonry are also a reflection of yet another truth: there are only three discrete "degrees" existing in the universe that are within man's perception and comprehension—the physical realm, intelligence and morality.

Freemasonry speaks in symbols and teaches the eternal principles of morality. The truths of its philosophy teach us what God and nature are, and what we are, and lift us into a sphere of intellectual independence and religious freedom. Toleration of diversity is one of Freemasonry's greatest "secrets." Without it, men of differing beliefs could never act in one brotherhood under the Fatherhood of one God, as Freemasonry has done always. Triune symbolism teaches us the certainty that God disinherits none of His children, but permits all to call Him Father.

KNOWLEDGE:
A MASONIC DUTY

"Bow down thine ear and hear the words of the wise,
and apply thine heart unto my knowledge."
Prov. 22:17

Freemasonry teaches that each man possesses a Divine and human nature, represented by the triangle. Human nature is depicted on one line of the triangle, the Divine on another and earthly matter on the third. Knowledge, or the relationship of each side of the triangle to each other side, is symbolized by light. Ignorance is symbolized by darkness. When a candidate for the various degrees of Freemasonry declares his desire to enter into the mysteries of Freemasonry "in search of the light," then later declares his desire to "search for more light," he literally means that he is there to acquire knowledge.

To learn, to attain knowledge, to be wise is a necessity for every truly noble soul. To teach, to communicate that knowledge to others is equally the impulse of a noble nature and the worthiest work of man. The monuments of genius and learning are more durable and lasting than the monuments to power. These maxims, as well as others found in Freemasonry encourage Masons not only to learn what has been set forth by our Masonic writers, but to also seek the light elsewhere.

Learning is a Mason's duty, because by acquiring knowledge man prepares himself to serve his neighbor, his brother, his family, his country and his God. To attain that which is unknown to others and to keep it locked tightly within our hearts is akin to place a lamp under a bed where it cannot shine. The noblest destiny of every Freemason is to take that lamp from beneath the bed and let it shine for others to see. What one man knows will likely prove helpful to another either to solve a personal problem or fathom a great philosophical expression.

Our Nations' Founding Fathers, several of whom also happened to be Freemasons, were mostly regarded as "Renaissance men," that is men who were learned in the arts and sciences. Diversity of knowledge was their character and the imprint of that diversity may be seen today in the symbolism associated with the original architecture in our Nations' capitol. Every culture, religious thought and ancient truth is commingled, memorialized and seamlessly blended. Search the obelisk that is the Washington Monument. Study the columns supporting the Capitol Building. Witness the grandeur on display at the several Smithsonian Museums. Each piece to the puzzle stands separately, but is seen as a whole and harmonious system.

Freemasons are not required, or even asked to become the smartest, brightest and best. Rather, Masons are simply taught the virtue and joy of learning. Each person progresses at a different pace, displays different interest, expresses different talents and contributes a piece to the puzzle that is eventually answered—"serve your brother with all your might, with all your heart and with all your soul."

A POINT: THE BEGINNING OF GEOMETRICAL MATTER

"For God,…commanded the light to shine out of the darkness."
2 Cor. 4:6

In Masonic teachings, a "point" is used to symbolically illustrate several truths. The point within a circle is intended to convey (1) the eternity of God, and (2) the circumscribed boundaries of one's behavior. When applied to the more esoteric concepts arising out of the study of geometry, the "point" alludes to a man's potential. Fellowcraft Masons are instructed that a point is the beginning of all geometrical matter. Rather than simply accepting that obvious fact, Freemasonry asks us to look deeper into the meaning of that symbolism.

Throughout the studies in Freemasonry, references to "above" and "below" repeat themselves. The manner in which the square and compasses is arranged within a lodge is a prime example: the square is pointed downward, or to the "below," while the compasses is directed upward, or at the "above." Hermeticism has long taught that the "above" and "below" signify the conjoining of Divine will with human purpose. In Freemasonry, the most important goal to which a Mason aspires is to be entirely in sync with the Great Architect; to align human will with Divine will and thereby serve all mankind with the greatest loving kindness imaginable. In alchemy, that conjoining of wills constitutes the correct mystical blending of the infinite with the finite mind—the illumination of darkness with supernal light which has no beginning and no end.

While God endures forever and is not confined by the dimension of time, such is not so for man, who being a part of the material world has a material beginning and a material end. The "point" symbolically demonstrated in Freemasonry is also meant to imply that there is a starting point for man's understanding of and relationship with God. For some, it is at the knee of a devout parent; mother, or father. For others, it begins after years of ritualistic attendance at religious houses of worship. And yet for others still, the commencement of a relationship with God begins during the evolution of understanding that results from a prolonged exposure to Freemasonry. Regardless of the path, the result is usually the same: man begins an earthly journey in the light.

It is that light which enables man to see the truths lying in wait behind the various arrangements of symbols in Freemasonry. The greatest of these is the truth that there is life after physical death. Consider the "raising" in the Third Degree; contemplate upon its meaning and understand the truth it conveys. Freemasons are also informed from lessons in that degree that an acacia should remind us that we are each invested, by virtue of our creation, with a spirit or affinity that will never die.

Consider the potential, or starting point, illustrated by the Third Degree of Freemasonry. A Mason is free to abandon his personal point of view, to renounce his personal will at any time during his life and to feely follow the wisdom taught by the Supreme Architect of the Universe. A Mason truly has no greater obligation during his material lifetime.

WHENCE CAME YOU?

"And behold, I propose to build an house
unto the name of the Lord my God."
1 Kings 5:5

Masonic catechism replies to the question "Whence came you?" in the following manner: "From a Lodge of the Holy Saints John at Jerusalem." From the Jewish historian Josephus, we are informed that when he captured Judea, King David renamed the city "Jerusalem." As we also know, King Solomon's Temple, like the Tabernacle erected at Moses' command, was situated due east and west—a geography that lends revealing information about why the city was named "Jerusalem." Far from a mere historical lesson, the reason touches upon the essence of a specific belief system that delivered us Hiram, King of Tyre and Hiram Abif who together with Solomon are considered Freemasonry's first three Most Excellent Grand Masters.

The first known form of name for the renamed city was "Urushalim"—"uru," meaning "founded by," and the suffix "salem," or "Shalim," which is the name of the ancient Canaanite god of Venus in its evening setting. Interestingly, both Hiram of Tyre and Hiram Abif were Phoenicians and Canaanites. Thus, the very name "Jerusalem" effectively means the place dedicated to Venus in her evening setting.

However, Solomon's Temple faced the opposite direction toward Venus rising in its role as "Morning Star." That is so apparently because of the importance of the Sun's symbolical association with the Divine. It is also true, because the "Shekinah," or presence of the Divine, was visible only in the east as a pre-dawn astronomical phenomenon. Astronomically, "Shekinah" represents the concurrence of Venus and Mercury, which is exceedingly rare and does not occur with mathematical precision.

Using state-of-the-art computer software, technicians have recently "dialed back" the time clock to learn what was present in the skies during certain notable events. Surprisingly, the "Shekinah" phenomenon was present on the dates attributed in history to the exodus of the Jews from Egypt; at the building of King Solomon's Temple; and, during the time attribute as the birth of Jesus.

The Ancients placed great religious significance upon Venus, variously describing the luminous planet as the manifestation of the female component of the Deity (an attribute arguably continued by the Catholic Church in its Story of Mary, the "Mother of God"), the symbol of fertilization, and the Light of Divine Glory. Ancient Canaanite worshippers, as well as Egyptian mystics and early Druidic societies astronomically "timed" the appearance of Venus' light in the eastern pre-dawn skies and calculated roughly 40 year intervals between the appearances. Coincidentally, the number "40" occurs exactly 40 times in the Holy Bible.

The Temple of Solomon was constructed with a dormer, that is a small window situated in a position whereby sunlight could be let inside the Sanctum Santorum. That light was also referred to as the "Shekinah" and shone upon the Ark of the Covenant, which remained inside the Holy of Holies until the Temple's complete destruction by invaders. Solomon adopted Hiram of Tyre's reverence for the Divine Light, secured it for Israel, and caused it to dwell in the Ark at Jerusalem. The lineage of that belief system traces itself directly to both Saint John the Baptist and Saint John the Evangelist—two eminent patrons of Freemasonry.

THE PRINCIPLE OF BROTHERHOOD

"A man that hath friends must shew himself friendly: and there
is no friend that sticketh closer than a brother."
Prov. 18:24

The principle of brotherhood and the obligation of a distinct
affection for fellow members are characteristics common to many
fraternal organizations. Too often brotherly love is, in reality, treated
as a mere abstraction, an indefinable something that is not truly
practiced. In many instances, if it is practiced at all, the individuals
involved are motivated by selfish interest, such as manipulating
others to give aid, or to be made to feel guilty for refusing.

A candidate for degrees in Freemasonry, however, will likely
discover that the tenets of brotherly love, relief and truth taught him
are regarded by the Craft "Masonic ornaments," that is the sheer
foundation of an institution built upon the great principle of love.
The mode and manner of the practice of these principles is detailed
in words which are illustrated in symbols so that there may be no
cause for error in understanding, or failing to practice. No Mason is
likely to forget the "Five Points of Fellowship" or the interesting
incidents that accompany their explanation; and, as long as he is
controlled by his knowledge and retains this memory, he is not likely
to fail in his duties of brotherly love.

Benevolence is sometimes defined by other Masonic writers as the expression of goodwill to others which results in great deeds of kindness. It is prompted by the emotion of love inculcated in the divine command: "Thou shalt love thy neighbor as thyself." A benevolent disposition suffers uneasiness at the suffering of others, abhors cruelty under every guise and pretext and seeks to relieve those conditions. It becomes universal when it yearns for and strives to secure the welfare of all men—friends and enemies alike.

Freemasons are taught to look upon all mankind as having been formed by the one Great Architect of the Universe in a spirit of love and sympathy. They are also taught to discharge the duties of benevolence in the widest and most generous scope. Masonry is an internal principle intended to regulate outward conduct. Masons are encouraged to become essential—to work for the benefit of others, to labor for our neighbor's best interest, to never become satisfied that we have given enough, but to pray for the strength to ceaselessly be a brother.

IN UNITY

"Behold, how good and how pleasant
it is for brethren to dwell together
in unity."
Ps. 133:1

Freemasonry recognizes certain inalienable rights of men of every race, creed and religion to have different opinions about all of the vital issues of life, including, but certainly not limited to, the freedom of thought and liberty of conscience. Genuine unity in mind and heart, as well as in the noble purposes of Freemasonry, is urged upon Masons at all times. True brotherly love and fraternalism are cultivated and a community of interest among the brethren of the mystic tie is maintained at all times.

That tie emerges from the vows of eternal brotherhood professed at the altar by each Mason. It binds Masons to brotherhood regardless of race, religion, or social affiliations. Freemasonry's devotion to these, as well as other tenets of virtue, has remained steadfast throughout times of greatest stress, including the American Revolution and American Civil War. The voice of the Masonic leadership in each era resonated with urgings to work for peace, to stay law abiding, to be tolerant and to be free. Those Masons expressed a concern to their followers that remains relevant today: our greatest enemy does not approach from without, but from within.

In his book entitled "The Fire from Within," Carlos Castenada writes: "Self importance is man's greatest enemy. What weakens him is feeling offended by the deeds and mis-deeds of his fellow man. Self importance requires that one spend most of one's life being offended by something, or by someone." Freemasonry promotes the virtue of considering every other brother as another self. When that state of existence is achieved, not only in the mind, but also in deeds, it is impossible for self-centeredness to survive. With the self as the focal point, one sustains the illusion that he or she is, in fact, his or her own body –an entity completely separate from all others. It is that sense of separateness that leads men to compete rather than cooperate with others.

It is essential that Freemasons maintain a strong self-concept and feel appreciated. One does not have to abandon himself altogether to also appreciate another brother as another self. Consider the fact that having achieved the state of looking upon others as another self when one does not treat himself very well—when one behaves badly, acts dishonestly, or engages in other destructive conduct. Unless the other person is offered honesty and virtuous treatment, he or she can do quite nicely without the attention.

A problem also arises when one misidentifies who he or she truly is by simply identifying himself or herself as a body shape, a body size, by the type of goods possessed, by the number of personal achievements gained, or by a personal dogma. Mankind's gravest conflicts and wars have resulted primarily from an insistence that one point of view was more accurate than any other.

Since Freemasons voice approval of such virtues as charity and justice, it is imperative that each Mason conduct himself consistent with love and fairness toward all whom they meet. When self importance spins its vicious web and disharmony results, if a Mason is present it becomes his indispensable duty to work to promote cooperation and compromise. When someone else states differently it is important that the Mason hearing consider before responding that it is not necessary that he always be right regarding every subject abut which he, too, has an opinion. When a Freemason stops to contemplate how he has spent his life, if he has acted upon the lessons taught him, he would discover that he had served God with a purpose. And when all is said and done; when the soul returns unto God who gave it, the best reward of all would be to hear those gentle words, "well done, my son—you have served my unity."

THE FATHERHOOD OF GOD

"So God created man in His own image, in the
image of God created He him; male and
female created He them."
Gen. 1:27

Freemasonry teaches that man is the offspring of God by creation; that God made mankind to be of one blood; and, that God's fatherly love for man finds its greatest expression in His redemptive plan for "fallen humanity." Religions will disagree one with the other about the precise nature of that plan, but none dispute that a plan of redemption does, indeed, exist. Freemasonry stays away from such disputes and permits each member to lean upon the religious faith of his choice for further understanding about the plan of redemption.

However, the lessons of Freemasonry temptingly lure us to ponder the deeper esoteric reason why God would care.

When all is said, we are truly a pitiful race. We kill each other; starve each other; permit poverty to weaken us decade after decade; and, we barely tolerate a neighbor who fails to see religious matters the same way we see them. Yet, in spite of our shortcomings, we are constantly informed that each one of us is God's special child.

Borrowing generously from ancient Hermetic thought, certain Masonic writers have postulated that God cannot help but love us, both the good and the bad, because we are one with Him. Some insist that the Divine and human intellect are identical; that what some refer to as the Holy Spirit actually lives in our minds, which some consider to be the seat of man's soul. This notion is not peculiar to Freemasonry and Hermeticism. In fact, the same sentiment can be seen in the writings of many so-called self-improvement authors, as well as in the writings of Albert Pike himself. Consequently, in that the notion is repeated throughout time and by men and societies of differing backgrounds and dogmas, it has begun to acquire a certain status of truthfulness among all men.

As Pike observed, "...all Light is one, so all Intellect and Reason being one; each Human Intellect a minute ray of the Infinite Intellect." [Pike: Lectures on Masonic Symbolism.] Can such thinking be merely the result of human vanity and conceit, or is there a further basis in truth for literally knowing that we are, each one of us, a part of God?

Justin Martyr, a Roman Catholic, wrote during the middle of the second century that the doctrine of the unity of God is above all other doctrines. Indeed, until Irenaeus wrote in the latter second century about the theology of dualism (God existing separately and apart from man), most of those who are referred to as the Ancient Fathers promoted the belief that God, the all-being cause and creator of everything, existed in the soul of man and acted as man's conscience. Literally, that meant that God and man were one, or at least of the same essence. The ramifications of such thinking are enormous and lend further credence to the lesson attributed to Jesus—that all men are capable of achieving the highest spiritual state of "sonship" with the Father.

Today, we often hear Masonic speakers refer to Freemasonry as, "A brotherhood of man under the Fatherhood of God." It matters not if you accept a unitarian point of view, the concept of dualism, or even notions of pantheism (God existing in everything, everywhere). It only matters that you recognize the great truth that God is, and you are because He is. As such, you are no more important and no less important to God than is your neighbor.

The important duties you owe to God, your neighbor and yourself may be found in the "Volume of the Sacred Law" (Holy Bible). When read often, it reveals how essential it is for each of us to be forgiving, nurturing, tolerant and loving. When any of those virtues are lacking in us as individuals, others with whom we have contact are deprived of intercourse with God. Indeed, when those virtues are lacking in us, we contribute darkness rather than light to mankind's collective soul and fall short of fulfilling our Masonic vows.

HUMILITY OF THE MIND

"Before destruction the heart is haughty.
And before honor is humility."
Prov. 18:12

The Holy Writings teach us that all is vanity and in so doing enlighten us to the fact that worldly pleasures are fleeting and end in emptiness. A thoughtful man who considers his life's toil cannot help but reflect upon what he has wrought, what works he has accomplished, and what treasures he has accumulated. One preacher and sage observed that when he looked at all of the work of his own hands and considered the extent of his own labor, he actually saw that all was vanity and vexation of spirit—that nothing that he had wrought on his own profited him anything of lasting value.

The various rituals employed in Freemasonry teach us that all brethren should maintain freedom from pride and arrogance. It is most destructive to view oneself as wisest, most faithful, most industrious and more important as a result of a more talented nature. The good seed of harmony spread by others is thereby choked by the weeds of our own self importance. Freemasonry's ritual also teaches how much can be gained by relying upon others to also exert their unique and equally important talents; how society is so much more benefited by the working together of multiple hands and minds. The initiate for Masonic degrees does not conduct himself around the lodge room—he is assisted by others. He observes not only one pillar in the lodge—he sees no less than three. The administration of a lodge is not committed to the care of one man—a line of officers work together for the greatest good of the whole.

The first step toward acquiring any truth is to adopt a humble mind, a sense of personal ignorance, and a thirst for knowledge to use for the benefit of ourselves and others. We live in an age of ever increasing fanaticism, intolerance and rage seemingly driven by an unrelenting and crazed certainty on the part of the fanatics that they alone act in the name of God. It is the height of vanity for anyone to presume that his or her perception of God constitutes the sole and complete truth; that others who disagree are so subhuman as to deserve a swift and vengeful demise.

The well known Masonic writer, Albert Pike, once observed that, (T)he Mason does not dogmatize, but entertaining and uttering his own convictions, he leaves everyone else free to do the same; and only hopes that the time will come, even if after the lapse of ages, when all men shall form one great family of brethren, and one law alone—the law of love—shall govern God's whole universe." [Pike: Magnum Opus.] The correct path is pointed to in the first of God's Ten Commandments delivered by Moses to the Hebrews: "…thou shalt have no other gods before me." That directive may only be accurately understood by a humble heart and mind, a spirit so subdued to God's will as to faithfully know that He created everything, not simply some things, and that He loves everyone, not just some, regardless of the religion they adopt, or chose not to adopt. When we sincerely believe that He wishes all, not merely some, to live in complete peace and harmony, we have, indeed, taken the required first step toward attaining "truth."

The prayer spoken by a humble mind does not presume that the Great Architect is like Santa Claus—someone to be called upon only when we wish Him to do something for us. Rather, the prayer spoken by the humble mind seeks to know God, to be like God and to serve His will by knowing His knowledge—the knowledge of brotherly love and affection.

THE FAITHFUL SERVANT

"When thou vowest a vow unto God, defer not to pay it;
for He hath no pleasure in fools; pay that which
thou hast vowed."
Eccl. 5:4

All Freemasons are required to be steadfast in keeping the vows of the Order. That is so, among other reasons, because Masons are expected to be sincere in the practice of all the virtues taught by the ritual, symbols and lectures. Masons are further expected to maintain unflinching loyalty to the fraternity in the manner of a faithful servant.

A faithful servant is one who keeps his vows, is diligent in his stewardship, behaves dutifully to his Master and remains loyal in the face of trial and tribulation. In the explanation of the ritual used in the Entered Apprentice Degree, faith is said to be the first rung of the theological ladder employed in Masonic education. Trust in God is required and is accordingly emphasized in each of the three degrees of Freemasonry. That trust constitutes the basis of true character and service, and thus demands a belief in something beyond ourselves, beyond science and beyond our capacity to know anything at all for certain.

Masonic ritual continually verifies the virtues of faith and trust and teaches Masons everywhere to conform their personal conduct accordingly. Candidates for Masonic degrees are blindfolded, not for the purpose of frightening them, but to teach them a valuable lesson about trusting in one who is there to guide. In the Entered

Apprentice Degree, the candidate is reminded to fear not what man can do unto him, but to exercise faith that the brother guiding him will not permit him to suffer harm.

The lessons about faith and trust are not intended to remain limited to placing such in the hands of a brother. They are also intended to teach the candidate, as well as the Freemason already arrived at his Master Mason status, to permit God to lead him throughout life. One of the first questions asked of a candidate is in whom he places his trust. The response is one of the most important vows made in a Mason's career: the vow the trust in God.

The manner in which Freemasons respond to their duty to their country, their neighbor, their families and themselves evidences the true extent of their faith. How a Freemason responds to calamity, misfortune, ill fortune and the reality of his own death demonstrates the extent of steadfastness he possesses. The true measure is what others may see in the response—not what is intended, but what is actually done by the man himself. One may have the best intentions about how to behave and fall short when the time to perform arrives. To so fail is part of human nature. Theology refers to such conduct as "sin," because it is conduct that separates man from God. Yet, to fail means to have tried. And, having once tried, to try again and again and yet again without ever losing faith that the trust in God will eventually erode much of what makes us fail.

It is within our human nature to be fearful, doubting and questioning about our own faith. Man searches frequently for proof of the truth about that which he is asked to believe. That, too, is human nature. Yet, when Jesus was asked by the masses for a "sign," he responded by stating that the generation would receive nothing more than the sign of Jonah. What was meant by that saying was that man will repeatedly find that God helps him, that God is always present when He is called upon and that He will ever be a faithful servant to His Creation. We are merely asked to believe that to be true—to exercise faith and trust, which require each of us to rise above our human nature and satisfy our souls that God is truth and that nothing we have ever attained in a secular education has ever disproved His love for us.

A FREEMASON'S ATTITUDE TOWARD ADVERSITY

"Rejoice with them that do rejoice: weep with them that weep."
Rom. 12:15

Times of ill fortune or destitution, whether of the purse or the soul, touch the lives of every Freemason, his family and friends. It is, indeed, the mystery of this earthly existence that all mankind is destined to suffer, not because the Great Architect has willed us pain, but that we should learn important lessons about life. Poverty, ill health, times of war, moments of self doubt, persecution, fear and death itself extends ugly tentacles and threaten to grip us is a vice of depression. We have, each one of us, experienced the very best, as well as the very worst that life has to offer. Along the way we have learned that the best hope we have in coping with the very worst is the love and comfort of our families, our friends and our Masonic brethren.

Masonic tradition teaches us that such adversity must be accepted cheerfully as a test of our character and met head on with prayer and courage. We are also taught to go to the aid of a brother who is in the grasp of despair and to seek out other brethren when we ourselves are in need of comfort. Yet, to do so we must first know our brother.

A brother neglected is never truly known. A brother who is not forgiven his faults and errors does not truly exist. A brother upon whom we have turned our backs is not permitted entry into our lives.

If giving and receiving comfort in times of adversity is a Masonic characteristic, Masons must often meet with their brothers, frequently speak with their brethren and easily forgive a brother a real or imagined trespass.

Anger, disharmony, or pain suffered as a result of past injustices too often influences a man to forsake another, for one brother Mason to ignore another worthy brother. When we allow such evils to separate us, who will be there to rejoice when we rejoice, or to weep when we weep?

Doubt not that such evils exist, even within the halls of a Masonic lodge. Cain first struck his brother killing him on the spot. That one uncontrolled departure from brotherly love resulted in the separation of two brothers forever. Instead of prospering and living a life full of loving emotion, Cain was compelled to wander the earth with a burning conscience. Yet, that story from the Holy Bible is but one example. History will not soon forget the holocausts, the infanticides, or the incessant march of men filled with hate from one generational war to the next.

Healing begins at home with each man's God, his family and his worthy brother Mason. If you harbor ill will against anyone for any past slight, wrong, injury, or injustice, try to be the first to pick up the telephone and call that brother. Time is running out and you may never again have the chance.

The time will come when we shall all meet again in that Great Celestial Lodge above where no man is less than any other, except the one who failed to forgive his brother. Forgiveness is a divine virtue, for every day God forgives us much, or He would not permit us to live. Prepare for the adversity to come by forgiving the brother in front of you. You will need his comfort, as he will need yours.

HISTORY vs. MYTH

"The sun shall be no more than the light by day;
neither for brightness shall the moon give light unto thee
but the Lord shall be unto thee an everlasting light,
and thy God thy glory."
Is. 60:19

It has been said that one of the fallacies of conventional scholarship is to insist on a rigorous and artificial distinction between history and myth. According to that distinction, "history" is regarded as documented fact, or data that will withstand assorted tests and scientific scrutiny and prove that something actually happened. On the other hand, "myth" is routinely dismissed as irrelevant, or incidental to history. Too often, "myth" is consigned to the realm of fantasy, poetry and fiction. When compared to the acceptance of history as fact, "myth" is relegated to the low rank of being a spurious embellishment, or falsification of fact. Yet, many of the most educated of the "Ancients" drew no distinction whatsoever between the two, more often than not simply referring to both as accurate recollections of past events.

Events described in the Old Testament of the Holy Bible, such as the parting of the Red Sea, or God meeting Moses face-to-face to give him the Law, are held by many people today to be mythical stories. But, there are also many who believe those same events actually occurred. In truth, there is much that is referred to as history that simply cannot be proven to have occurred. For example, the "facts" allegedly recorded by the great Jewish historian, Josephus, are littered with inaccuracies owing primarily to the inclination of Josephus to reflect a specific bias, or perspective about the politics and culture of his age. Most historians of that same era, as well as throughout later generations sought to convey how they respectively saw the events unfolding around them without regard to the truth of the recorded facts. Those "histories" are clearly biased and inevitably falsify or distort what actually transpired. For example, speculation surrounding the events leading to the assassination of President John F. Kennedy, or even the actual whereabouts of rock star, Elvis Presley, is variously couched as either historical or mythical depending upon who is telling the story.

Inquirers after Masonic truths have for ages vainly attempted to separate and distinguish history from myth as the two schools apply to the beginnings of Ancient Craft Freemasonry. Some of Masonry's most learned men continue to debunk one author, or another, because a particular work is not actually "history," but merely unproven "myth." Yet, in so doing, Masonry's greatest minds unwittingly tend to deprive the rest of us from a specific form of "light" and threaten to leave unread valuable information that may actually assist us to understand what Freemasonry truly means to the world, as well as to its individual members. If the Ancient Craft is nothing more than the sum total, or result of a sudden eruption upon the world scene in 1717, how do we account for the numerous rich symbolic stories, legends and "histories" about the glorious Temple of King Solomon? Why does Freemasonry devote entire degrees to Moses? Why do the twelve tribes of Israel play such a significant role in the organization and conduct of Masonic Lodge meetings? And, why do we continue to demonstrate a resurrection of the soul as a part of our Masonic ritual?

Historians have never interviewed the deceased to actually record how each is faring after life on Earth, yet all Masons fiercely believe in an afterlife. History has neglected to record where God came from, what He is doing, or why He cares anything at all for mankind. Yet, Masons express a zealous belief in His existence. In other words, there is much that Freemasonry claims to "know" to be true for which there is no recorded history. Indeed, much of what is "known" is informed by the soul of man—matters of faith that some would refer to as fantastic, imaginary, wishful thinking, or "mythical."

Much that is written about Freemasonry qualifies as myth, but it should neither be rejected outright, nor adopted as having actually occurred without a critical review. All that is written, whether history or myth, is intended to inspire, to influence the heart and soul, and to spark a thirst for more Divine Light. Just as the workmen at the Temple of Solomon initially threw away the stone that would prove most valuable to the construction of the edifice, we risk so doing if we reject one form of information in favor of another. It is more likely the case that the spirit that resides within each of us knows the difference and can be trusted to teach us the truth.

TWO THINGS WORTH LIVING FOR

"The labor of the righteous tendeth to life;
the fruit of the wicked to sin."
Prov. 10:16

Writers about Freemasonry have told us that there are but two things worth living for: to *do* what is worthy of being written, and to *write* what is worthy of being read. The greater of these is the *doing.* No matter how magnificent and noble an act an author can describe, or the artist paint, it is far nobler for one to go and do that which one describes, or be the model which the other draws. In other words, when we pause to look within ourselves to assess how well we are doing in living life, the standard by which every Freemason measures his past, present and future worth is his work and the example he sets for others to follow.

Freemasonry teaches that contributing to the best interests of our fellow man is the noblest work of mankind. In the great Providence of God, in the great ordinances of our being there is opened to every man a sphere for the noblest action. More often than not that sphere is not of extraordinary heights. Rather, it is borne of the exemplification of extraordinary virtues displayed during an ordinary life. It arises most often during times of silence and seclusion, in wearing sickness without complaint, displaying sorely tried honesty that asks no praise and privately yielding advantage to another.

It is natural that all men should desire distinction. But those who seem happiest are those who seek to develop beauty. Such is the true harmony of the universe. Here below, each Mason has a work to do in himself greater than any work of genius; a work upon a nobler material than marble, or stone—a work to be created and completed upon his soul and intellect.

A great author or artist only portrays what man should do, both virtuous and commended to our mutual admiration and imitation. Yet, the practical realization of the great ideals of art include the exercise of love, piety, truth and all that is right. They are displayed in the daily routine of ordinary lives and survive as testaments to the true character of a Freemason.

Duty is always with us and forbids idleness. To work with the hands or brain according to each person's skill and capacity is more honorable that either title, or privilege. When one considers the world in its primitive creation, it is easier to understand that God was wise to give us a dark mass with which to work; an empty canvass upon which to draw the character of man's existence. Mankind is, therefore, taught and encouraged to create as God creates, to love as He loves and to add beauty to His beautiful bounty.

When time has finally run its course and we conclude this wondrous journey on earth, among our survivors who will honor the memory of the riches we have accumulated? Who will recall that we lived a life of luxury? Who will want to recount the deeds of treachery that drove us to the top? Such things are but vanity and will wash away in our dust. But that which we do for others will live forever.

THE MYSTERY OF CREATION

"The heavens declare the glory of God: and
the firmament sheweth His handiwork."
Ps. 19:1

Freemasonry recognizes one great "Creative Architect" in the
origin of the world and the vast expanse of solar and planetary
systems. For each individual Mason, the Earth and the heavens are
living symbols of God's own handiwork and declare his glory. The
mysteries of creation revealed in the various symbols of
Freemasonry are the foundation for each Mason's personal
relationship with our Divine Creator.

From time immemorial, our Ancient Craft has accepted the
account of creation recited in the Old Testament of the Holy Bible as
the revealed truth of God. Rather than constituting a literal truth, the
story told is a symbolic recitation Masons may ponder while
meditating more deeply upon the infinite nature of the Supreme
Architect of the Universe.

At several points during the history of the world, men of various
intents and purposes have hijacked the purity of such religions as
Judaism, Christianity and Islam to impose a man-made interpretation
of God's creation. To Hermetic Christians, this exercise of power by
man is an exercise of the power taught by the serpent to Eve in the
Garden of Eden, a theme that was repeated later in the Old Testament
in the story about the Tower of Babel. Each of those religions has
spawned numerous sects each in turn attempting to explain God's

infinite wisdom and power using only man's very limited finite knowledge.

To the contrary, Freemasonry adheres to the notion that such shortcuts in thinking inhibits and confines the true essence of our indefinable Creator and God. Even certain scientific thought, most notably Einstein's "theory of relativity," concludes that creation is not entirely subject to human explanation. Similarly, philosophers such as Plato have also concluded that human intellect alone is incapable of fully understanding the infinite windings of creation. Religious doctrines seek to fill the void left by the inadequacies of science and philosophy, as does Freemasonry, by inculcating a belief that the truth about the infinite can only be fully discovered and appreciated through faith.

As the purer religions of Judaism, Christianity and Islam once did, Freemasonry turns to certain symbols that reveal specific truths about the heavens and Earth. It is not by accident that Masonry interprets a special relationship among the twelve (12) sons of Jacob and the twelve (12) signs of the Zodiac where the planets are domiciled at various times throughout each year. For example, the Zodiacal lion called "Leo" (whose constellation resides with the Sun—Masonry's singular symbol of sovereign authority) relates to the Tribe of Judah. During Masonic ritual, Masons are taught the significance of the "strong grip of the lion's paw."

Similarly, Freemasonry has discovered that astronomy offers further proof of the resurrection and renewal of life in the seasonal activities occurring in the heavens. In late December of each year, the Sun recedes to its lowest point in the heavens, there to remain for three days before beginning its gradual ascent to its highest point in late June. This phenomena was interpreted by many of the Ancients as a Divine revelation that death (symbolized by the winter season) yields to renewed life (symbolized by the spring and summer seasons).

In much the same vein, Freemasonry teaches, through its use of selected symbols about creation, that the true "Temple," or inner spirit of man, is in a process of constant construction. Masons are instructed that the Supreme Architect of the Universe, having once dwelled at the Temple of King Solomon, now dwells in the Temple's true successor—the heart and soul of each man, woman and child. Because none of us are perfect beings, Masons believe that mankind is in a constant condition of refinement through the lessons of honor and virtue. In other words, mankind is in a perpetual state of creation that will never die.

THE AWAKENING

"O dry bones, hear the word of the Lord."
Ez. 37:4

From beginning to end, the rituals of Freemasonry symbolize and teach the doctrine of man's immortality and repute every iota of the doctrine of annihilation at death. This doctrine is at the core of the lessons taught in the Third Degree. A Mason's understanding about death is accompanied with no gloom, because he comprehends the truth that death is physical sleep for an unknown period of time, from which will spring an awakening of the body and a resurrection of the soul. Yet, as is so with all Masonic symbols, this, too, has other meanings for Masons to ponder.

In the Book of Genesis found in the Holy Bible, God and the serpent each have their say about life and death. On the one hand, God said, "Do not eat the fruit of the Tree of Knowledge, or you will die." On the other hand, the serpent told Eve, "That is ridiculous, you won't die." Here, it is important to understand whether or not the serpent simply lied to Eve, or committed fundamental error due to his misunderstanding. Stated differently, did the serpent actually state a truth found within the range of truths proper to his domain? Thus articulated, we are asked to consider whether or not there are two immortalities at issue in the Book of Genesis, as well as two different deaths—one from God's perspective and another from the serpent's point of view.

Our scant empirical experience with death reveals that it is the disappearance from the physical plane of other living beings. But, there are other disappearances within the physical plane which we call "forgetfulness," or "lack of knowledge." A core lesson taught by Freemasonry relates to the importance of knowledge to the welfare of every Mason. Therefore, even the symbolism of the resurrection should also be considered in that context, as well as in the more traditional context of immortality. In the whole of our experience, "forgetting," "sleeping," and "death" are three different manifestations of the same thing—disappearance.

One forgets, one goes to sleep, and one dies.

One remembers, one awakens, and one is born.

In addition to intellectual forgetfulness, there is also forgetfulness within the domain of the soul. An absence of faith, hope and charity shrivels the soul and darkens the spirit, moving man from the light to the darkness. Thus, it is the thoughts of the divine (symbolized by faith, hope and charity) which actually raise the consciousness of the human soul and propel it to work. Without charity, the soul is dead even though the organism within which it resides continues to breathe. It is reduced to animal and mineral qualities and bears little affinity or resemblance to that Supreme Intelligence which pervades all nature and which will never, never, never die.

Freemasonry asks each Mason to evaluate death by asking this question, "What do I myself really know about death?" That evaluation requires the use of one's memory, which is either mechanical, or moral. Moral memory is more effective, because it does not link the present to the past on a physical plane, as does mechanical memory. Rather, it links ordinary consciousness to spiritual consciousness—what is below to what is above—which is the source of our certainty about God, as well as our own immortality. Masons are taught to use their memories not merely for the purpose of regurgitating in their proper order the various words used in ritual, but to also teach the valuable lesson of expanding memory to different planes to attain a greater spiritual awareness about his own relationship to God and the universe.

THE SABBATH

"And God blessed the seventh day and sanctified it; because that in it He had rested from all His work which God created and made."
Gen. 2:3

Throughout Masonic ritual, especially the ritual of the Fellowcraft degree, the Divine appointment of one day of rest is firmly acknowledged. For the Hebrews, the Sabbath, or day of rest, was also a day of devotion to God during which no menial work was to interfere with meditations upon His greatness. In its esoteric context, the Sabbath represents something more; something essential to a world filled with grace.

Three historical personalities have vividly portrayed the idea of what is known as the "cosmic wheel," also known to Masons as the point within a circle. They are Gautama Buddha, King Solomon and Friedrich Nietzsche. Buddha saw the "cosmic wheel" as an open circle, or as Masons will recognize, a spiral staircase from which birth, death and suffering can pass into the soul's center of rest. Solomon saw the "cosmic wheel" as inexorable fate rendering vain all human hope and endeavor—the emptiness of the world which can only be filled by God. Nietzsche saw and understood the "cosmic wheel" as a fully contained universe with no outlet—a world of eternal repetition into which no new light could shine. Nothing can be added to, or taken from Nietzsche's world. It is infinite and determinable; literally a world without God. However, in the world of both Buddha and Solomon, we notice something much different.

Although Solomon preached sadness and despair as man's lot in material existence, something inside of him defined a deliverance from woe long before Christians hailed Jesus as the Messiah. So, too, did Buddha, as well as the Hebrews themselves when they instituted the Sabbath at Moses' instruction. By the exercise of the Divine wisdom granted him by God, Solomon believed that the material world was spatial and consisted also of an as yet uncreated part. That belief was based upon Solomon's wise perception that God's infinity had a place in the already created finite world as a continuous realm of creation. That uncreated part is symbolized by one day of rest, or the Sabbath, which in Solomon's interpretation was the opening in the "cosmic wheel"—the path by which miracles occur and new life is created.

The worlds of Buddha and Solomon can be transformed. Nietzsche's cannot. A closed circle implies that there is nothing new under the sun; a cosmic hell. An open circle implies that there is an entrance and an exit to this world and that there is no eternal prison. Solomon believed that God was not unknowable, but rather knowable through the exercise of inexhaustible infinite knowledge. That is precisely why he encouraged his constituents to study, research, build and unceasingly work. The concept that we may, each one of us, come to know God's infinity is the very essence of the eternal neverending Sabbath, symbolized for us as the seventh day of creation. The Sabbath is laden with possibilities of new beginnings, new causes, new journeys and new endings. From it energies can be added to the so-called constant quantity of the phenomenal world, just as energies of this world can disappear in it.

Like Solomon's constituents, Masons are also taught the value of an unceasing search for knowledge, not solely to acquire learning, but to use it to the greater glory of our Creator, as much as to the welfare of our fellow creatures. As Masons, we understand what our Most Excellent Grand Master knew: the open circle in the "cosmic wheel" means that we will always have something new to learn.

FEAR AND INJUSTICE*

"Love ye therefore the stranger: for ye
were strangers in Egypt."
Deut. 10:19

*[This article originally appeared soon after the 9/11 attacks in New York]

In this hour our Nation cries out for the soothing touch of Masonic values necessary to fill a terrible void resulting from a horrific fear that engulfed all who watched newscasts repeating with numbing regularity the awful sight of jumbo jets piloted by men with wicked intent tearing into New York's highest landmarks and sending them crashing to the ground as though they had never before stood in their place. In the aftermath, the people were left in stunned confusion fearing that others in their midst also intended immediate harm and acts of evil. As the reporters around the globe scanned the emerging pictures of those who piloted the planes, repeated their names and read their biographies, entire communities began to fear anyone among them who looked like the evildoers, or shared similar sounding names. Soon, reports about unwarranted harassment of such people flowed across the various news wires, as Americans everywhere tried to cope with thoughts of shadowy enemies stalking this great nation. It is a new age event, but sadly it is also an old age phenomena.

This attack was not the first on America. Our history is checkered with similar episodes with hateful events resulting in reservations for

Native Americans, internment camps for American Japanese, horrifying lynching's of African Americans and the destruction of lives and careers during the era of "McCarthyism." Neither is this the first time Freemasons have been reminded of their duty when faced with such widespread community fears. Grand Masters from numerous states orated at the outset of our Civil War about mankind's need to pause and reflect. Brother Franklin Delano Roosevelt called upon a nation beset with unsettling uncertainty during the Great Depression to endure and thrive, boldly declaring during one of his famous fireside chats, "we have nothing to fear but fear itself."

Freemasonry echoes the same sentiment which derives from the essence of its ritual, educational literature and personal experiences in fraternalism. Our fraternity has witnesses the scourge of persecution prompted by fear. Masons should know that fear begets intolerance and that in turn intolerance begets tyranny. Throughout history, Masons have stood witness to injustice, torture and death inflicted upon mere whim, or because people thought differently, dressed differently, spoke differently, or worshipped differently. Freemasonry feels the pain of the generations of human beings who struggled mightily against oppression. Some tasted only a gruesome death as their earthly reward. These are the true enemies of mankind. Like the shadowy terrorists lurking in darkened caves and tunnels, they, too, lurk in the darkest recesses of a fearful heart.

It is said that no man is entirely without fear all of his life. Sooner or later all men become afraid of something. Masons have been provided working tools with which to combat any fear that may threaten to overwhelm. They are taught to practice charity toward everyone, not just those with whom they best get along. They are also instructed to circumscribe unruly desires and keep passions within due bounds, not only toward those whom they like, but also toward those whom they may not even know. Masons are expected to render justice universally, to extend mercy freely and to compassionate every man's misery. They do not promote fear and suspicion, but act to bring all such fears into the light that in knowing the source man is prepared to chase away such demons. In the military terms of our age, these are a few of the "smart bombs" that can be launched in man's battle against ignorance, intolerance and fear.

In the same manner in which our monumental buildings have become targets of terrorism, so too have our moral values. If we acquiesce in the unjust treatment of our neighbors simply because we fear their names, their religion, or their place of origin, we have been defeated by hatred, anger and fear. The Holy Writings make clear to us that it is far easier for man to love his friend than to embrace his enemy. Freemasons are not given an option—love thy neighbor means exactly that regardless of who or what is your neighbor.

Throughout history bigotry and hatred habitually filled the void left when a whole society permitted itself to wallow in fear. Recall the tales from that period of time known as The Inquisition. Recall how in the 20th Century an entire people were led to believe that annihilation of the Jews was necessary, proper and moral. Recall how educators, politicians and business leaders were demonized because they once inquired about communism. Such is the result of cowardice, weakness and fear. Masons must do better. The fraternity must rise above the mob mentality, reacquaint itself with its values and lead the march toward justice for all, not just those whom we do not fear.

The Masonic mission in this hour is clear: in words and deeds Freemasons must stand united in the renunciation of unfair harassment of any man, woman, or child solely on account of one's name, place of origin, color, or religion. When the voice of bigotry is heard in the streets, the Masonic voice of unity must rise higher. When hatred bubbles to the surface in social intercourse, Freemasons must openly plant seeds of kindness. When one person suffers unjustly in the presence of a Mason, the entire Craft has failed.

By doing your duty when the going gets rough, a Freemason not only lives his values, he demonstrates that his moral fiber is tough, sturdy, resilient and unbending. Stay strong, my brothers, for this, too, shall pass and our fraternity will be scrutinized by others intent upon showing to the world that Freemasonry is hypocritical—that it stands for values it does not practice. Your oaths and vows demand that you never allow that to happen.

THE FIRST GREAT LIGHT

"...I have found the book of the law
in the house of the Lord..."
2 Kings 22:8

The symbols studied in Freemasonry reveal the many truths surrounding the concept of the Trinity and, among other ways, conceal them within the number "3." The number "3" may at some times represent the Triune God, at others the three states of harmony, and yet on other occasions the three primary "trunks" of the Tree of Life. Equally central to Masonic thought are what is termed the "Three Great Lights of Masonry;" the Holy Bible, square and compasses. The first and greatest of those lights is the Holy Bible, or as is often said, "The Holy Writings."

Freemasonry does not promote any one formal religion or belief system over any other and therefore tolerates the use of Holy Writings other than the Holy Bible. The Torah and Koran are excellent examples. If at any time the Craft of Freemasonry concludes that one book is more fully inspired than any other, Masonic Law provides that is sufficient reason for selecting the one found to excel. In most American, English and European lodges, the Holy Bible is selected. In California, regardless of which Holy Writings are selected, the Holy Bible must also appear alongside upon the altar.

Many, if not most symbols used in Masonry are taken directly from the scriptures contained in the First Great Light, or Holy Bible. The virtues and morals promoted by Freemasonry are also interpreted from its teachings. As such, the Holy Bible is regarded as the symbolic revelation of the very Word of God, which if ever lost will leave mankind in utter darkness.

In Masonic ritual, the brethren are also taught that if the Word of God is ever lost, it is an absolute Masonic duty to recover it through arduous research, intimate inquiry, meditation and prayer. Indeed, a significant part of Masonic ritual emphasizes the fact that even though the Word of God is available in the form of the Holy Bible, if man determines never to read its pages, the Word is as good as lost, for it is never learned. Therefore, the Masonic duty referred to is one of consistent reading of the scriptures and prayerful reflections upon their meaning.

The loss of the Word of God may also be viewed in an historical context, which further veils the concept of Divinely radiated truth. Certain Masonic ritual reveals that during the so-called Babylonian Captivity, the Torah and scriptures were lost to the Hebrews, but was later discovered when they returned to Jerusalem and commenced construction of the Second Temple. Paulinian Christianity teaches that the Word, present to the world in the person of Jesus, was again lost when Jesus was crucified only to be yet again rediscovered through the inspiration of the Holy Spirit. Other Masonic ritual further incorporates this same notion of loss in the portrayal of that celebrated artist who was murdered.

In each instance, the inescapable lesson for every man is to pursue the truth with fervency and zeal. Among Masons, the adequacy of that pursuit is measured by the extent to which the individual progresses from initiation through full development in the mysteries of Freemasonry. The Holy Bible, or First Great Light, is the definitive symbol of Divine Truth. The system of belief each man selects as his "religion" will dictate for him how he will interpret that truth. Freemasonry asks its members to understand that all such systems of belief have some merit and therefore should be studied to enable the individual Mason to synthesize and in so doing to assist the spiritual evolution of all mankind.

SECRECY AND SILENCE

"Even a fool, when he holdeth his peace,
is counted wise: and he that shutteth
his lips is esteemed a man of
understanding."
Prov. 17:28

Contrary to popular belief, Freemasonry is not a secret society though it has been railed against as such during various periods of volatility in world history. Neither does it seek to conceal its existence from the rest of the world. The names of the membership may be known to all who are interested. Every state within the Nation has a Grand Lodge of Freemasonry and a website on the Internet. One need simply make a keystroke and there you have before your own eyes a full display of all who proudly wear the honor of being a Freemason. Too, many Freemasons wear easily identifiable jewelry as a further display of their membership in that honorable institution. The element of secrecy applies solely to the ritual used in the degrees of Freemasonry, the manner in which one brother Mason may know another, and to the interpretations of the various symbols and legends made use of during Masonic education. The tenets and truths that Masonry teaches are as open to the world as though Masonic meetings were town hall events rather than carefully "tiled" (carefully secured) events.

Yet, even though it is not a secret society, Freemasonry does regard secrecy and silence as necessary safeguards against those who wish to bring down the fraternity. To speak of such is not at all paranoid when one pauses to recall that a king and a pope conspired to burn Masonic ancestors at the stake and wipe them from the face of the earth. Precisely why that occurred is not the topic of this article, but it is illustrative of the reason secrecy and silence enjoys a place of respectability in the Order. Perhaps equally important is the fact that Freemasonry instructs in the same manner as one would pursue a comprehensive study of mathematics. Before one can comprehend algebra, he or she must learn to add and subtract. For a period, algebra is "concealed" until the proper building blocks are in place to insure that the best chance to learn the truth about algebra is present.

The improper use of certain Masonic "secrets" by the uninitiated could seriously detract from the fraternity's message about charitable brotherhood, undermine the credibility of the many truths embodied in fraternal doctrine and unjustly injure the reputations of hundreds of thousands of virtuous brethren. Therefore, while an uninitiated person may justifiably inquire about the origins of Masonry and its virtues (some writers have alluded to the actual discovery of early Masonic scrolls containing great truths about God that lie hidden beneath the floors of King Solomon's Temple, pointing to those discoveries as the genesis for adopting secrecy and silence), the wisdom for demanding secrecy and silence for certain matters is indisputably correct.

By requiring the exercise of secrecy and silence about the mysteries of the Order, Freemasonry follows principles that were in place in all of the ancient mysteries and systems of worship of the Deity. The Egyptian and Judaic priestly orders are excellent examples. In Ancient Egypt, no "profane" was ever permitted into the ceremonies that instructed men about the resurrection of the dead. In the Judaic culture, only the High Priest was permitted into the Sanctum Santorum, or Holy of Holies situated within King Solomon's Temple. He was the only person within that society who could speak the ineffable name of God once a year into the ear of an initiate while loud music prevented it being heard by anyone else.

If you study well, you will learn that there is nothing sinful, immoral, or contrary to the laws of God about such requirements. To the contrary, secrecy and silence wisely anticipate that holy knowledge derived from ritual and symbolism may best be understood by a candidate for Masonic degrees who is guided along his Masonic journey by serious minded "elders," who point him in the direction of the correct path. Masonic requirements of secrecy and silence also serve to safeguard that ritual and symbolism as pure "vessels" of truth to be sipped from during the presentation of the degrees as fine wine. If one is worthy of becoming a candidate for Freemasonry, he need only knock and the door will be opened unto him. He need merely ask and he shall receive all of the mysteries he proves worthy to receive. Those who choose not to knock and not to ask have no need to view the contents of Freemasonry. They would not be understood by a faithless heart.

If you seek further justification for Freemasonry's rules of secrecy and silence, consider also this fact: multitudes of thousands of men of the highest intelligence, of the most enlightened ranks and of the most profound piety have, without compunction of conscience, obeyed these rules for hundreds of years. As a result of that faithfulness, it remains possible for a true and enlightened heart of faith, hope and charity to beat within the soul of every Freemason.

SO MOTE IT BE

"But without faith it is impossible to
please Him: for he that cometh to
God must believe that He is, and
that He rewards them that
diligently seek Him."
Heb. 11:6

Masonic prayer frequently concludes with the ancient phrase spoken by all Masons in attendance, "So mote it be," which is another way of saying: "The will of God be done." Or, it is also a way of acknowledging that whatever be the answer of God to a Mason's prayer, so be it—the answer will always be wise and correct.

This ancient phrase has at least two meanings. First, it represents the assent of every Mason uttering it to the will of the Supreme Architect of the Universe. He is counted wise and brave who, baffled by the trials of life when disaster follows fast, can nevertheless accept his lot as a part of the will of God and say, though it may be difficult to do so, "so mote it be." Secondly, the phrase also represents the assent of God to a Mason's aspiration. We can endure many hardships, perhaps anything, as long as we feel that God knows, cares and feels for us. These two meanings constitute elements of a Freemason's true faith, emblematically represented in Masonic ritual by the first rung of that theological ladder, which Jacob in his vision saw reaching from earth to heaven.

Perhaps the best indications of a Mason's faith in the Supreme

Being are his acts of prayer, as well as the manner in which he prays. The simple act of prayer demonstrates a hopeful reliance and repose in the unknown and further shows a belief in and pursuit of immortality. It also denotes Freemasonry's universality and connection with the laws set forth in the Holy Writings, as well as our belief in God, which every man must openly express before he can be made a Mason. To be effective, this simple act of prayer should be coupled with the proper prayerful attitude, or manner, which does not include begging God to merely do what it is we want Him to do. The proper attitude is one of humble contemplation which leads us to do God's will and not our own.

The role of prayer in the work of Freemasonry is not perfunctory. It is not a mere matter of form and rote. It is vital and profound. As an initiate enters a lodge room, prayer is offered for him to God in whom the initiate is instructed to place his trust. In a later Masonic degree, during a candidate's figurative condition of crisis, the candidate must pray for himself, either orally or mentally as he prefers. These specific acts of prayer are not simply ceremonial— they each constitute the basic faith and spirit of Freemasonry.

A Mason should never be ashamed to pray. When all is said, prayer is a part of the sanity of life. It refreshes the soul and clears the mind. Oftentimes there is more wisdom in a whispered prayer than in all the libraries of the world. God knows our needs before we speak them to Him. Yet, we ask of Him anyway, if for no other reason than to become better acquainted with our best Friend.

Grant us, Almighty Father of the Universe,
Ardently to desire, wisely to study, rightly to
Understand, and perfectly to fulfill that which
Pleases you.

So Mote It Be!

LABORARE EST ORARE

"The labor of the righteous tendeth to life:
the fruit of the wicked is sin."
Prov. 10:16

Operative Masons labored at the building of stately material edifices. We who now call ourselves Speculative Masons are taught the importance or working to erect a superstructure of virtue and morality. Each one of us is aided in that task by the principles conveyed to us in our various lessons in Freemasonry.

From first to last, Freemasonry is *work.* The institution venerates the Supreme Being, oftentimes referred to as the Great Architect of the Universe; commemorates the *building* of King Solomon's Temple; employs emblems fashioned after *working tools* used by masons and artisans; and preserves the name of the first *workers in brass* as one of its fraternal passwords. When brethren meet together, they are said to be *at labor.* The Master of a Lodge is figuratively seen as the overseer who *sets the Craft to work* and gives them the necessary instruction whereby they may proceed in their *labors.* Thus it is that Freemasons everywhere are consistently instructed that there is a perennial nobleness and sacredness in *work.*

There exists in both philosophy and theology a distinction between static concepts and fluid *work.* The static, or closed universe that exists without change, ignores the great truth that God is a creative force. He is the beginning, the present and the future. The ineffable word is said to be His true name and regardless of whether one adopts the Greek, the Latin, the Islamic, or the Hebrew pronunciation, God is change. Change comes from *work*, which improves upon the static, placing it into constant motion.

In addition to this truth, Freemasons are also reminded of yet another truth: *faith without works is dead.* From time immemorial, Freemasons have been invited to look within themselves, to study religion and philosophy, and to meditate upon the great goodness of our Great Architect of the Universe. But for Masons, that alone is insufficient to support their status in our world as *practical philosophers.* There is no virtue without activity and exertion, whether physical or mental. To learn for the mere sake of learning is useless, because the gift—that which was learned—is not passed along to others by the action we know and refer to as *labor.*

The *work* referred to herein is both literal and philosophical. It was well that God gave the earth to man as one dark mass whereon to labor. It was also well of Him to provide rude and unsightly materials in the ore-bed and the forest for him to fashion into splendor and beauty. It is better for the Mason to work while he lives than to simply enjoy life as it passes by; to live richer and to die poorer. Our Christian brethren will well remember the Sermon on the Mount and the lesson that one who gives everything of himself is truly blessed. It is best of all to banish from the mind that empty dream of indolence and indulgence.

A Freemason routinely addresses himself to the business of life and considers it the school of our earthly education. He has also settled the question for himself that as a man of freedom and independence, gained by the sweat and toil of his ancestors, he is far from exempt from *labor.* Masons build; they are in motion; they promote change; they create; they imitate their God in every manner possible.

THE SQUARE AND COMPASS(ES)

"And it was in the heart of David my father
to build an house for the name of the
Lord God of Israel."
1 Kings 8:17

Knowledgeable Masons quickly recognize the Square and Compass, two of the Great Lights of any Masonic Lodge. In combination, they constitute the oldest, simplest and most universal symbol in Freemasonry. They are so recognizable as literally symbolizing Masonry that years ago, when a business firm attempted to adopt the Square and Compass as a trademark, the U.S. Patent Office refused permission on the ground that, "...there can be no doubt that this device, so commonly worn and employed by Masons, has an established mystic significance which is universally recognized." Indeed, nearly everywhere in Masonic ritual, as in the public mind, the Square and Compass are seen together as never being far apart. Since the Compass is an instrument composed of two arms, some Masonic jurisdictions refer to it as a "Compasses."

It is elementary to even the youngest Entered Apprentice that the Square is an emblem of morality, and that the Compass teaches men to circumscribe their desires and keep their passions in due bounds toward all mankind. While Masonic interpretations are well known, tracing the origin of Masonic use of these symbols is much more problematic. To simply attribute Masonic use of those instruments to tradition is not at all satisfying to the inquiring mind. As is so with most symbols in Freemasonry, nothing definitive is written about the Square and Compass in Masonic history. Therefore, one is required to use logic and intuition in conjunction with what Masonic history that does exist to discover the probable truth.

While some may disparage conclusions necessarily based upon a belief that the Knights Templar were "founders" of Freemasonry, it is undeniable that in today's Craft, Freemasonry honors Knights Templar and, likewise, Knights Templar venerate Ancient Craft Masonry. Thus, some well recorded early Templar history is useful when considering the origin of the Square and Compass.

One of the oldest symbols known to the ancient Knights is the Seal of Solomon, also more popularly known as the Star of David. The Seal held special significance to the old warrior monks, accounts of whom are articulately set forth elsewhere in writings by prominent Masonic authors. Since Bibles were generally unavailable during the Middle Ages, it is deemed quite likely that the ancient Templars took their oaths while placing their right hands upon the Seal.

Even before the French and Papal persecution compelled the fleeing Templars to institute secret "modes of recognition" as a life saving measure, the old Knights veiled the deeper meaning of relevant symbols, such as the Seal, in allegory. (Interestingly, Freemasonry, too, has adopted allegory as its tool of secrecy, providing yet another piece of evidence that the Templars and Freemasons have some common source of origin.) In its most recognizable form, the Seal appears as two interwoven equilateral triangles. Being equilateral, each side of each triangle is of the same precise length as each other side. The secret meaning of the Seal would correctly have been veiled to appear one way to the outside world, while representing something quite different to the initiated. For example, consider many of Da Vinci's artworks, the most famous of which is "The Last Supper." To the initiated, the character pointing heavenward with his index finger has a very significant esoteric meaning. The uninitiated simply sees it as a finger pointing upward.

To view the symbol Masonically, thereby completely changing the Seal's appearance, nothing more is required than omitting the horizontal bars from the interwoven triangles. If you draw the remaining figure for yourself, it should not escape your notice how similar the symbol is to Freemasonry's Square and Compass. Although not definitive as to its origin, by any means, this similarity may not simply amount to random coincidence when it is recalled that each institution venerates the other.

In order for the occurrence to be a coincidence, it would also have to be a coincidence within a coincidence. For, if you have drawn your figure correctly, you will note the position of the "legs" of the "compass" derived from the Seal, with one "leg" above the "square" and one beneath it. That precisely copies the position of the Square and Compass as it is used in the Fellowcraft Degree, which was once regarded as the degree of full membership in the brotherhood of Freemasons.

Assuming that the Square and Compass was derived from the Seal, it is also logical to wonder why the Seal would have been so significant to ancient Templars. The use of the Seal, or Star of David, as a Jewish symbol is of fairly recent vintage. Early rabbinic literature has found no historical support for the claim that it represents the shape of King David's shield, as once was thought to be true. Nevertheless, the interwoven equilateral triangles have appeared in very ancient literature and artworks, some pre-dating the arrival of the Templars.

Wholly apart from Judaism, the symbol was quite common during the Middle Ages as a sign of good fortune. Furthermore, various scholars have identified a deep theological meaning hidden within the symbol: the top triangle strives upward toward the Supreme Architect of the Universe, while the lower triangle strives downward toward the real world. That symbolism is common in Hermeticism— "as it is above, so shall it be below." When accepted in this context, Freemasons will surely recall the fraternity's special call for universality which permeates all Masonic ritual.

If the Holy Bible is the rule and guide of our faith, as all

Freemasons are taught, the Square used as an emblem of morality in conjunction with the Compass representing regulation of conduct consistently displays implications of universality. Is it not so that the three Great Lights of Masonry suggest, promote and inculcate faith, hope and charity? Nothing can be more universal.

THE 47TH PROBLEM
OF EUCLID

"Bow down thine ear, and hear the words of
the wise, and apply thine heart unto
my knowledge."
Prov. 22:17

Master Masons are instructed that there are a series of hieroglyphic emblems about which they are expected to inform themselves. Simply defined, a hieroglyphic emblem is a pictorial representation that is intended to convey a specific knowledge. One of those emblems is the 47th Problem of Euclid, authored by Pythagoras, an ancient friend and brother who in his travels throughout Asia, Africa and Europe was initiated into several orders of Priesthood. He was also raised to the sublime degree of Master Mason.

Pythagoras was also schooled in Hermeticism, the tradition of synthesis that explains the divine concept of "as above, so shall it be below." Hermeticism teaches that man should seek to apply the infinite wisdom of God to the finite environment in which he resides on earth. As a student of that tradition, Pythagoras' scientific explorations were as much the result of his search for divine truth, as they were a quest for mathematical reality. To him, mathematics was the core of divine order in the universe. Therefore, the principles of the celebrated 47th Problem of Euclid constitutes a key to Masonic geometry, not only with respect to external forms, but also with regard to the moral and intellectual powers and capacities of man.

The matter of the 47th Problem is this: if any triangle has one right angle, the squares of the two shorter sides, when added together, will contain precisely the same area as the square of the longer third side, also known as the "hypotenuse." The Problem establishes the clear relationship that exists among length, breadth and thickness. The triangle unites the squares which when applied to Freemasonry symbolizes the unification of the three lodges of the Entered Apprentice, the Fellowcraft and the Master Mason into one complete whole. Thus, it is a perfect picture, or hieroglyph representing the perfection of the three degrees of Masonry when considered together.

Various historians have suggested that the application of the 47th Problem of Euclid resulted in the precise form of the Tabernacle of Moses, as well as the form of the Holy of Holies standing within the Temple of King Solomon. Closer inspection by several Masonic writers reveals that it also provides the true form of both the Master Mason's apron and the jewel worn by the Worshipful Master. As a consequence, when a Mason sitting in a Masonic lodge views those symbols, he is reminded that taken together, they represent that order and beauty which reigns forever before the throne of God.

Also for consideration by the contemplative Freemason, the understanding of this celebrated Problem is central to an appreciation of the relationship of one degree of Freemasonry to all other degrees. They are each building blocks without which the other two would be without form. When it is noted that the world was first without form and void, the 47th Problem of Euclid may also be seen as a figurative formula for the "DNA" that scientists have recently come to recognize as central to life itself.

Before a Mason can achieve the "perfect square" of a Master Mason, he must have first proceeded along the oblong paths of the preceding degrees. In other words, he must evolve according to the knowledge that he acquires. The "perfect square," emblematic of truth and morality, may only be acquired after absorbing the progressive lessons in virtue offered in the symbols and lectures of the Entered Apprentice and Fellowcraft degrees. Once those lessons are entirely understood, the Master Mason is sufficiently equipped of spirit and mind to see the truth of Freemasonry's venerable mysteries. Thus, even a Master Mason should once in awhile return to study the lessons taught in the preceding degrees to make certain he has learned all that he should.

Freemasonry also looks to the 47th Problem of Euclid as a basis for concluding that all philosophical and religious thought is worth consideration and respect. The Problem teaches that any one particular perspective about God is not incorrect, or correct. Rather, it represents where the person holding that belief is in relationship to mankind's evolving understanding about man's relationship to the Deity. As humans, we cannot know whether that place is advanced or retarded—we may only regard it as the place one is in his or her understanding about his or her relationship to the divine. Therefore, all places are to be respected, because they are all divine, at least in some part.

THE LETTER "G"

"O Lord our Lord, how
excellent is thy name
in all the earth."
Ps. 8:9

One of the most familiar, as well as most significant symbols in Freemasonry is the letter "G," which is always visible in the east suspended above the Master's chair. Masonic tradition explains that this symbol has at least two very profound meanings. First, it is the initial of the name of the Supreme Architect of the Universe—the great God of all Masons. Second, it also represents geometry, the science by which the labors of all artificers are calculated and formed. For Masons, geometry contains the determination, definition and proof of the order, beauty and wisdom of God's creation.

The great Pythagoras concluded that the mathematics of geometry, so precise and unerring in the theorems to which it gives rise, was also intended to inspire mankind with a spiritual knowledge. That knowledge, that all of God's creation from beginning to end has a clear, carefully calculated plan that adheres to a specific set of reliable rules, is something Pythagoras was certain that man was able to decipher, if he studied and meditated properly. His belief is consistent with the several passages of scripture found in the Holy Bible which teach us that there is nothing that God will not reveal to His children. The sole requirement is that the children ask for such knowledge with a pure heart.

Thus, in its dual symbolism, the letter "G" represents to Masons the creative genius of God, His unity with creation, the unity of heaven with earth, the unity of the divine with the human and the unity of the finite with the infinite. The latter was the subject of Albert Einstein's "relativity theory" about which he first wrote in 1905. In further contemplation of those truths, Freemasons everywhere engage in common acts of charity and refuse to accede to the undervaluing of this life as being somehow insignificant; worthy only as a stepping-stone to a future heavenly existence. To the contrary, Freemasonry teaches that devotion to God and that which is above includes devotion to all earthly life, especially to the causes of virtue and social justice.

The letter "G" also serves as a reminder to each Freemason that life is real, earnest and full of duties yet to be performed. In sum, Masonry propounds that life is the beginning of immortality and is meant to be commanded and controlled, not neglected, despised, or ignored. The measure of a man's devotion to God, virtue and duty is taken by evaluating his various actions toward others. That measure does not count idleness, the pursuit of self interest, or the useless wringing of self-pitying hands. Such attributes are found only in the pagan, or heathen heart—the breast in which God dwells only in name, if he dwells there at all.

BOAZ AND JACHIN

"And he set up pillars in the porch of the Temple:
and he set up the right pillar. And he called the
name thereof Jachin: and he set up the left
pillar, and he called the name thereof Boaz."
1 Kings 7:22

The above quoted passage of Holy Scripture alludes to the erection of two huge shafts, or pillars of bronze, within King Solomon's Temple by Hiram, a man of Tyre and the son of a widow from the tribe of Napthali. Those pillars stood in relief as works of art, not as supports for any part of the structure itself. Boaz stood on the left and Jachin loomed on the right of the entrance to the Temple, just as they do today within every Masonic Lodge. As works of art, Boaz and Jachin were originally intended to serve as symbols of the unification of strength and virtue. They also represent a unification of Hebrew and Canaanite religious practices symbolized by the very persons of both Solomon, King of Israel and Hiram, King of Tyre.

Boaz signified "strength," while Jachin, a derivation of two Hebrew words, "Jah," the poetical term for Jehovah, and "Iachin," meaning "establish." Taken together, they mean "God will establish." Used in prayer set forth in the various Masonic writings, they become emblematic of the Supreme Architect's eternal loving power: "O, Great Architect. You are mighty, and your power is established from everlasting to everlasting." As one gazes upon the representations of Boaz and Jachin within a Masonic Lodge, one should also try to see the invisible arch connecting them to be none other than the hands of God.

The ancient Order of Melchizadek established a holy priesthood to serve as God's hands on earth. That priesthood continued through to the Hebrews, eventually to a person symbolically named "Zadok," who is intended to represent the continuity of the priesthood established by God. Viewed separately, Boaz and Jachin individually signify the "kingly" and the "priestly" characteristics of the Deity and inspire us with a due reverence for His works. Christianity holds that Jesus joined those two characteristics unto himself, thus becoming for his followers both King and High Priest of the Order of Melchizadek.

The ancients utilized similar pillars to represent the unification of diverse people into one spirit. In the days of Abraham, the Egyptians erected one pillar in Upper Egypt and another in Lower Egypt to symbolize the uniting of the vastly disparate people of high standing, on the one hand, with the people of low standing on the other hand in the pursuit of one government and one religious truth. The people from both regions were polytheistic, as were most people of that era. They selected different "gods" and attributed greater or less significance to each as they chose. None fully believed that the others string of gods was either properly aligned, or equally powerful with their own. Yet, in spite of those vast differences of opinion, history clearly implies that the Egyptians realized that compromise, toleration and attempts to achieve harmony were greatly important to the welfare of the government and to the happiness of the individual.

Freemasonry acknowledges the tremendous contributions by the Ancient Egyptian culture to both civilization and religion. It emphasizes many of the concepts held dear by those Egyptians as fundamental to a just society. A population that seeks to accommodate different beliefs and permit the open expression of different opinions will more likely than not live peaceably. To the contrary, a population that rigidly excludes any but the selected beliefs and opinions will likely descend into civil war. Such has been the history of our world from time immemorial.

As Freemasons acting in today's societies, let us remember the true significance of Boaz and Jachin: God has said, "In strength will I establish this my house and kingdom forever." That strength derives from the solidarity of the people, which in turn derives from the loving, kind, tolerant respect one displays to another. It derives from the Masonic principle of "synthesis," or the ability to live side-by-side in peace and harmony with those who neither think like us, nor look like us.

FROM DARKNESS
TO LIGHT

"Then, God said, 'Let there be light', and there was light."
Gen. 1:3

Prior to the commencement of each ritualistic degree in Freemasonry, the candidate is placed into a symbolic condition of darkness. There, he discovers that he must rely upon other senses than sight to comprehend what is transpiring. More particularly, the candidate is encouraged to learn how to first conceive God's truths in his heart before beholding the beauties of His creation with the eyes.

In that Freemasonry has also equated the condition of darkness to being in a state of evil, or living in ignorance, it is important for the candidate to also learn the relationship between right reflection and correct action. That is, when one absorbs a specific subject matter, it becomes a part of that person sufficient to influence physical acts. By learning to so read and absorb the lessons taught by God's revelations about what is good and what is bad, the Mason enables himself to develop an instinctive ability to act according to what is right, that is in the light.

The Entered Apprentice Mason is instructed to consider the volume of the Holy Writings as the "Great Light" in his life; to regard it as the unerring source of truth; and to govern his actions by the Divine precepts therein contained. Anyone who has taken the time to read passages therein knows that they must be read slowly to be understood. That is so, because the concepts expressed about our living God are so sophisticated that they are best understood by the "heart," that is, the soul of man. In fact, once the heart has been conditioned to understand those passages, the eyes can actually take in the words at a more rapid rate. They are but the lens through which the soul of man sees, hears, and absorbs God's most elegant truths.

In the First Degree of Freemasonry, the candidate also learns that the "covering" of a lodge, the clouded canopy or star-decked heavens, is intended to remind him to have faith in God, hope of immortality, and charity toward all mankind. Therefore, the "light" to which Freemasonry alludes radiates most brilliantly when emanating from faith, hope and charity, which further illuminates the truth about the resurrection from physical death. If death is darkness, then life is represented by light. Eternal life is represented by eternal light—that radiance from above that so pervades everything as to forever eliminate the darkness. Thus, eternal light is the appropriate symbol for the immortality of the soul.

The Holy Writings, or "Great Light" in Freemasonry, also teaches that just as a body without a soul is dead, so also is faith without works. In its simplest context, that truth means that it is not enough for a man to believe that God loves all His children. To know that God loves all and to hate your own brother implies that such a one walks in the dark, not in the light. It is not enough to simply know that charity is essential to the welfare of our fellowman, one must actively seek out opportunities to practice charity. Therefore, charity is the handmaiden of faith, because it constitutes the "works" without which faith is dead.

Masonic tradition informs us that every Masonic Lodge extends from east to west and from north to south to denote the universality of Masonry, and to teach us that a Mason's charity should be equally extensive. The arrangement and situation of a lodge itself is also a Masonic symbol; a source of great radiant light—one that acts as a constant reminder of that purity of life and conduct so essentially necessary to gaining admission into the eternal presence of our God.

CORN, WINE AND OIL

"[He causeth]…wine that maketh glad the
heart of man, and oil to make his face shine,
and bread (corn) which strengtheneth man's heart."
Ps. 104:15

Masonic tradition informs us that the wages of a Fellowcraft
Mason are corn, wine and oil; the corn of nourishment, the wine of
refreshment and the oil of joy. If we do not inquire further into the
true meaning of this combination of symbols, it is likely that we will
overlook the deeper Masonic message it conveys.

Antiquity teaches us that corn was a symbol of the resurrection,
which is at the heart of lessons taught us in the ritual of the Third
Degree. Oil was anciently regarded as a symbol of prosperity and
happiness. In the Jewish tradition everything appropriated to the
purpose of religion in both the Tabernacle of Moses and Solomon's
Temple was consecrated with oil to foster public rejoicing and
festivity. Corn, or bread, was oftentimes used as a symbol of life, for
it was by bread that man sustained his physical existence for the
purpose of developing his spirit and soul.

Corn, wine and oil are also the elements used during the
consecration of new Masonic Lodges to dedicate the new Lodge to
the service of the Great Architect of the Universe. Writings by
several esoteric Freemasons reveal that angelic powers are released
within a new Lodge at the moment of consecration which can guide
even the most unwilling Freemason along the path of righteousness

and service to mankind.

The less mystical Freemason can appreciate a different interpretation of this combination of symbols on a more material level. As an emblem of food, corn reminds us that we are nourished by bread and the hidden Manna of Righteousness; wine, the emblem of refreshment, reminds us that we are to be refreshed daily with the Word of God; and oil, the emblem of Divine anointing, informs us that we are to rejoice with joy in the riches flowing from God's grace.

In that charity is regarded in Freemasonry as the "greatest of the three principle rounds of Jacob's ladder," which extends beyond the grave throughout all eternity, Freemasons will do well to also understand the lesson to be derived from this combination of symbols about how we are to treat others. The carrying of corn, wine and oil in a procession to consecrate a new Masonic Lodge may remind us that in the pilgrimage of life, we are to give bread (corn) to the hungry, cheer (wine) to the sorrowful, and consolation (oil) to the sick and afflicted.

As is true with most matters Masonic, the wages of a Fellowcraft Mason are not intended to be hidden away. They are to be displayed in the light and given away free of charge to all we encounter who are in need. In so doing, Freemasons participate in the continuing creation and offerings of love practiced by our Great Creator.

THE LOST WORD

"In the beginning was the Word, and the Word was with
God, and the Word was God."
John 1:1

According to the mystical history of Freemasonry, there once
existed in the ancient craft a Word of surpassing value. It has been
described as the unpronounceable name of God. Known only to a
select few, its true meaning was concealed to such a great extent that
the meaning was eventually lost. Those who once possessed the
Word were rumored to have the ability to exert enormous power.

Moses was directed to speak it as a name to Pharaoh and it
appeared hundreds of times in the Hebrew books of different
periods. Masonic tradition informs us that when, as a result of falling
into disuse, the Word was lost, the original Most Excellent Grand
Masters of Freemasonry, Solomon, King of Israel, Hiram, King of
Tyre and Hiram Abif, the widow's son, adopted a substitute for
temporary use.

As with most symbols used in Freemasonry, this, too, is subject to
several differing interpretations. The lost Word is believed by many
to constitute Divine Truth. Hermetic Christianity teaches that the
whole of God may be known to those who know and understand the
ineffable name of God. Therefore, the pursuit of knowledge is
essential to the person who would know the Word and know God.

One form of such knowledge may be derived from learning what
God is, what we are and how everything relates to the whole. Though

mostly ignorant about his own essence, man has ventured throughout time to speculate about God's nature, to dogmatically define the Supreme Being in creeds, and even to hate those who will not accept a particular point of view about Divine Truth. Yet, true knowledge of God's Divine Essence is impossible. Nevertheless the numerous man-made conceptions about God are significant revelations of man's intellectual development.

Limited to our own finite conceptions, as well as the finite conceptions expressed by other men, Freemasons are to study other ideas, exchange differing points of view, and attempt to understand what is truly meant by the words unity, brotherhood and charity. This pursuit is not purely theological, but extends to all of the liberal arts and sciences—how each relates to the other and how the sum relates to our perception of one great and powerful cause of being.

Unity itself has proven to be a concept difficult to put into action. Though the same sun shines on the earth to yield a plethora of fruits, plants and animals, none of which are alike, yet each owing its existence to the same source, man finds it difficult seeing his neighbor as another self. As Freemasons, we are reminded by the symbolic mosaic pavement that we are surrounded by opposites; by the position of the square to the compasses that there is both light and darkness; and, by the trestle board that there is a correct path we should follow—the path of brotherhood. If Freemasons observe the lessons taught them, they will know to apply knowledge in a manner that acknowledges the inalienable rights of all people, of all faiths and of all creeds. The founding fathers of this great nation held such beliefs worthy of a revolution against tyrants who would compel men to their way of thinking and their way of life—an example of integrity well worth emulating.

God permits all to call Him Father, and He disinherits none of His children. If you believe, as some believe, the He exists apart from man, then you are compelled to act according to His laws and love your neighbor, as He loves all of us. If you believe, as yet others believe, that God exists with us and within us, then you are compelled to act according to the laws written in your hearts. Both beliefs dispose man to act upon the truth that as inhabitants of the same planet, we are to aid, support and protect one another.

Freemasons do not regard their neighbors as simply Hebrew, Christian, Moslem, Buddhist, Republican, Democrat, communist, or fascist. Those are creeds, religions and political labels that merely define points of view, some with which we agree and some with which we disagree. But, the man possessed of any such creed, religion, or political persuasion is still permitted to call God "Father," and is not disinherited by Him.

To whom, then, should go the benefits of our knowledge? They should be showered upon every man, woman and child, especially the poor, the widows and the orphans. Pray for justice to all of these, my brother, and you will have done God's work—you will have taken an important step closer to knowing the lost Word.

THE INDENTED TESSEL

"Now faith is the substance of things hoped for,
the evidence of things not seen."
Heb. 11:1

During the First Degree of Masonry, the candidate's attention is directed to the "ornaments of the lodge," consisting of the mosaic pavement, the indented tessel and the blazing star. The mosaic pavement is intended to be emblematic of human life checkered with good and evil. It teaches that all humanity is imperfect in the eyes of God—at once capable of great acts of charity, and also of terrifying acts of brutality and murder. Yet, while journeying through this vale of tears, incapable of escaping the terrors wrought by mankind, Masons are reminded by the symbolism of the indented tessel that man may be set free from those terrors by a faithful reliance upon Divine Providence, hieroglyphically represented by the blazing star.

Examples of the rewards of relying upon God are sprinkled throughout the Holy Bible. When warned by God about a vast flood, Noah acted and by doing so demonstrated that he was a proper object for selection by God as an heir of righteousness. When Abraham was called to pack up and leave his familiar surroundings for a country he had never before seen, he did so. God rewarded his faithfulness by entering into a covenant with Abraham to treat Abraham's descendants as heirs. Moses led an entire Hebrew population from Egyptian slavery by faithfully relying upon God. Righteous to the end of his days, Jesus taught that the Kingdom of God was found within every man who professed faith in God.

Freemasonry embodies the same truth in the symbolic lesson intended by the indented tessel. The candidate is taught that the beautiful tessellated norder or skirting surrounding the mosaic pavement is emblematic of the manifold blessings and comforts one may hope to enjoy by a faithful reliance upon Divine Providence. In other words, good conduct is rewarded by God when performed with the pure intention of serving God's purpose. This symbolism suggests to the discerning Mason that even suffering can be a "manifold blessing"—perhaps not for the suffering person, but certainly for those who have the privilege of acting to relieve that suffering.

Since the beginning of man's history, wars have been fought and lives lost for the purpose of ensuring that other lives were saved. Throughout the ages, men and women have intentionally sustained diseases incurable during their lifetimes to help comfort and assist those suffering already from the same incurable disease. The blessing that was derived was to a later generation, which discovered the cure because of the sacrifices made. An entire generation suffered through the Great Depression with little or nothing in the way of material comfort. Those who survived taught a new generation important lessons about thrift and the social responsibility for caring for those who cannot care for themselves.

The greatest secret of Freemasonry is grounded in the hope and belief in something we cannot ever "know" to an empirical certainty—life after death. Is life after death a "manifold blessing?" Is it something you, as a Freemason, "know" to be true? Is faith the basis for that "knowledge?" If so, you have also discovered the commonality between "knowledge" and "faith."

Masonic writers have scoured the ages examining the Egyptian Mysteries, the Mithraic Mysteries, Hebraic teachings, Greek philosophy, dogmas from the Orient, and Christian writings to understand the full extent of the steadfastness with which people who partook in each discipline dedicated themselves to faith in God. None had ever seen God's face, felt His breath, or heard His voice.

Yet, each believed He was the source of all that is good and dedicated themselves to practicing faithfulness and recording that faithfulness in the rituals that have been passed down from time immemorial.

Similarly, it is also by our faithfulness and dedication to Freemasonry's work on behalf of God that those who follow this era will acquire a better understanding of God's loving kindness. Indeed, brethren, each generation of men is an "indented tessel;" a manifold blessing and comfort to those who follow. Man's opportunity to contribute to the welfare of generations that will follow is God's truest and finest gift to each of His creatures.

FREEDOM, FERVENCY AND ZEAL

"For he…was clad with zeal as a cloak."
Is. 59:17

As taught in the First Degree of Masonry, operative Masons were once required to serve their master with freedom, fervency and zeal. It was only in that manner that they could be certain to serve the master's interest instead of their own. In speculative Masonry, that same phrase is used to convey the notion that those three virtues are to be exercised whenever we serve the Great Architect. They are best demonstrated when our actions are consistent with advancing morality and by promoting the happiness of our fellow creatures.

Although Freemasonry states to the world that it is not a religion and does not promote any one established religion above any other, the Webster's New World Dictionary, Second Concise Edition, offers insight into why some insist that Freemasonry is a religion. The word "religion" is defined as "any object that is seriously or zealously pursued." Freemasonry has long had its accusers who state that the fraternity seeks to establish a "New World Order" under the banner of a new religion that will require its members to abandon Judaism, Christianity, Hinduism, Islam, or any other specific system of belief in and worship of God. To prove their point, some of those accusers cite various passages in the writings of esteemed Masonic philosophers, such as Albert Pike. In response, Freemasonry often argues that it is tolerant of all systems of belief and worship of one God and demonstrates that sincerity by extending charity to all regardless of race, creed, or religion.

Yet, as Freemasons it is important that we embrace rather than ignore, or try to conceal the fraternity's dedication to "zealously" tolerate, to love with "zeal," and to work for God as a "zealot." Pike has written that every Masonic Lodge is a Temple of Religion; its officers—ministers of religion; its teachings—instructions in religion. Pike so taught not because Freemasonry replaces Judaism, Christianity, Hinduism, Islam, or any other religion, but because Masonry promotes the duty of every Mason to adopt Masonic teachings and live them to the world through the religion of choice with enthusiasm, which is a synonym for "zeal."

Freemasonry teaches that there is, indeed, a "religion" of toil. It does not replace Abraham, Moses, Jesus, Mohammed, or any other great religious person. Rather it signifies that Masonry incorporates the virtues practiced since time immemorial which pervaded the thoughts and actions of each of those great leaders, as well as others. Masons are also taught that their pursuits and occupations, when performed faithfully, actually promote God's great design. Nothing less was taught by any of those great leaders. Masons are repeatedly reminded to advocate fairly and honestly with a feeling of sincere belief that it is God's justice that will prevail, not our own personal interests. Freemasonry further instructs that books, whether they are about Masonic history, philosophy, literature, or any of the arts and sciences convey a sense of "religion," if what is absorbed instills pure, noble, virtuous and patriotic sentiments. When he listens to what he is taught, a Mason learns that society itself, with all its diversification in belief systems, is a "religion" where, as here in our country, there exists a sacred belief in our fellow man, and where, again as here, we repose perfect confidence in the integrity of another person.

It is within the halls of the Temples, or Lodges, that Freemasons inculcate faith, hope and charity. With "zeal," Masons are taught disinterestedness, affection, toleration, patriotism, devotedness and an undying love of the Supreme Architect. Masons greet one another with joy; they are lenient to each other's faults; they carefully regard and respect each other's feelings; and, they are always ready to aid each other's wants and needs. That is the true "zeal," or as Webster has defined that word, "religion" which was revealed to the Ancient Patriarchs and which Freemasonry taught centuries ago. It will continue to be taught by Freemasons until time shall be no more.

If unworthy passions and selfish, bitter, or vengeful thoughts enter here, they are intruders within our Masonic Temple and most unwelcome. They are strangers and trespassers, not invited guests. If one is Jewish, these teachings resonate because they are also presented in the synagogues. The same is so if one is Christian, Hindu, or Moslem. Freemasonry seeks not to replace any one of those systems of belief. Rather, it seeks to bridge the gaps among them, to give to every human being the opportunity to learn with "zeal," regardless of the place of worship, or the system of worship employed. To Freemasons, there is only one God and we all live in His embrace.

TUBAL-CAIN

"The eighth man from Adam; the first artificer in metals."
Gen. 4:22

The Old Testament of the Holy Bible reveals that Tubal-cain was a son of Lamech, a descendant of Adam's son, Cain. He was described as an artificer in brass and iron. Masonic tradition embraces Tubal-cain as the founder of smith-craft, who likely worked in the implementation of metals into devices used for both war and peace. It is further speculated that he launched the Bronze Age, an historic era of enormous significance to mankind's ascent.

Many of the characters identified in the Book of Genesis who allegedly walked the earth before the time of Moses may not have actually existed. Many historians, both religious and secular, have come to the conclusion that most, if not all, represented either symbolic characters, or were composite characters, that is several people made into one being. That is particularly so with regard to Adam, Eve, Cain and Abel. In both the Kabbalah and Gnostic writings, each of those individuals is primarily regarded as a specific emblem of heavenly and earthly traits.

Cain and Abel are regarded jointly as examples of light and darkness, good and evil, while Adam and Eve represent both the earthly prototypes of man and woman, as well as the dual nature of God, in other words his active and passive being. If Cain is figurative only, so also may be his so-called descendant Tubal-cain, for history cannot definitely conclude that Cain and Lamech ever actually existed. As a consequence, Tubal-cain himself may be yet another in

110

a long line of Masonic symbols calculated to inculcate some type of spiritual awareness.

Within the various writings about Freemasonry there is a definite metallic streak associated with some of the Masonic ritual. As the Entered Apprentice will recall, he was divested of all minerals and metals before entering a lodge of Free and Accepted Masons. No tool of iron was used to assemble King Solomon's Temple. Chalk, charcoal and clay—extracts from the metallurgical process—are used to emphasize freedom, fervency and zeal. More specifically, clay is our Mother Earth which provides us with both the metals and the refractories to contain them at high temperatures. From charcoal we derive heat energy to smelt and refine those metals. From chalk we obtain the flux to alloy with the gangue then separate it from the ore.

Metallurgy as a science is closely associated with the philosophy of alchemy, which is to be distinguished from the so-called alchemical science. Scientific alchemy, or the changing of metal into gold, is largely disfavored as a pure science and more often viewed as a base form of magic. Philosophical alchemy, on the other hand, is very closely studied by Freemasons for its spiritual content. The "philosopher's stone" is the entire body of philosophic knowledge from which man's crude intellect grasps important truths about himself, his relationship to other human beings and his relationship to the Supreme Architect of the Universe.

Today's disciples of the symbolic Tubal-cain include tool engineers who provide the expertise necessary to design and devise the machines, methods and tools used to cast, forge and shape all metals. Therein lies a close association with Freemasonry, because all of the "working tools" are also essential to the fabrication of metals. For example, a tool engineer does not work without a rule, square, or compasses. Like Tubal-cain's art of metallurgy, this art also unfolds the secrets of nature and science teaching us what God and nature are, and what we are. God has provided us the materials in the firmament, the stars, planets and zodiacs, which we should be inspired to use to develop the knowledge necessary to accomplish our own Divine work.

Freemasonry instructs that most implements may be used by man for great good, or greater evil. Here, we return to the symbolic significance of the original brothers Cain and Abel, who begin the story of man with a lesson that our existence which is given us as a gift of our Great Creator is forever fraught with good and evil. The sharpened edge of an implement may cut stone to assist in erecting a house of worship. The same sharpened edge may also plunge deep into flesh and bone fatally wounding another human being. A mallet can serve to either join together parts of a building, or crush another man's skull. In each instance, the good or the evil results from the attitude of the person using the implement.

In the hands of a Freemason, the "working tools" are forged and malleated in his hands to eventually promote peace, goodwill, harmony, health and happiness. The mind of a Mason is disciplined by the lessons he is taught to employ the "good" attitude when using the tools and to turn away from the temptations to give in to the "bad" attitude. In other words, Freemasonry is about using ordinary substances to make gold; using his mind to serve his fellow man; using his soul to serve his God.

FREEDOM AND RESPONSIBILITY

"But God be thanked, that ye were the servants of
sin, but ye have obeyed from the heart that
form of doctrine which was delivered you."
Rom. 6:17

During the presentation of the First Degree of Freemasonry, the candidate is instructed upon the importance of freedom and the responsibility he has, as a Mason, to use it wisely. Freedom is the power, rooted in reason and will, to act or not act, to do this or that, and so to perform deliberate actions on one's own responsibility. By the exercise of free will, one shapes one's own life. Freemasonry teaches that human freedom is a force for growth and maturity in truth and goodness; it attains its perfection when directed toward God.

Yet, as Freemasonry also instructs, the world is made up of opposites, a truth that equally applies to the concept of freedom. As long as freedom has not bound itself definitively to its ultimate good—God—there remains the possibility of choosing between good and evil, and thus of either growing in perfection, or failing in wrong doing. The more one does what is good, the freer one becomes. Consider the example of our Grand Master Hiram Abif, whose habit of doing good cemented in him a necessity to always protect his integrity. His example also teaches that there is no true freedom except in the service of that which is just and good. Consequently, choosing to disobey and do evil is an abuse of freedom that inevitably leads to slavery of the human soul.

Freedom makes man responsible for his acts to the extent they are voluntary. Progress in virtue, knowledge of the good, and self discipline enhance the mastery of the will over its acts. Imputability and responsibility for an action can be diminished, or even nullified by ignorance, inadvertence, duress, fear, habit, or other social factors. However, every act willed is imputable to its author and even the best among us fall short. Consider that the prophet Nathan questioned King David after he committed adultery with the wife of Uriah and had him murdered: "What is this you have done?" All men are accountable and responsible for both the good they do, as well as for the evil into which they descend.

Freedom is exercised in relationships between human beings. Freemasonry recognizes that every person, created in the image of the Supreme Architect, has the natural right to be recognized as a free and responsible being. In many jurisdictions, Masons are referred to as "Free and Accepted" in further recognition of the dignity to which mankind is destined. Everyone owes to each other a duty of respect. Freemasons also recognize that the right to the exercise of freedom, especially in moral and religious matters, is an inalienable requirement of the dignity of the person. To become valid, this right must be recognized and protected by civil authority within the limits of the common good and public order.

THE FELLOWCRAFT

"Now therefore ye are no more strangers and foreigners,
but fellow citizens with the saints, and of the
household of God."
Eph. 2:19

Masonic tradition informs us that in operative Masonry there were
two classes of workers, Masters and Fellows. Fellows denoted those
men who were generally less skillful than those called *masters*. In its
etymological meaning, the word *fellow* signifies one bound to
another by a mutual trust; a follower; a companion; or, an associate.
In speculative Freemasonry, the man who ascends to the Second
Degree is referred to as a *Fellowcraft*. Like the Entered Apprentice,
the Fellowcraft is preparing to ascend to yet another and higher
degree.

While the First Degree of Masonry emphasizes the necessity of
purifying the heart, the Second Degree, or Fellowcraft Degree,
promotes the cultivation of man's reasoning faculties, as well as the
necessity to improve one's intellectual powers. In that regard, the
Fellowcraft is taught that Freemasonry is a struggling march toward
what is known as "the light." The Fellowcraft soon learns that the
march is not for individuals alone, but is also naturally pursued by
nations, or whole groups of people working together toward a
common goal. To give a nation the franchise of intellect, or light, is
the only certain way to perpetuate freedom. It therefore falls to each
Fellowcraft to learn, to obtain knowledge, to become wise and to

serve the interests of fraternal charity rather than self interest.

It is written elsewhere that the true Mason is an ardent seeker after knowledge and knows that both books and the antique symbols of Masonry are vessels which come down to us full-freighted with the intellectual riches of the past; and that in the lading of these argosies is much that sheds light on the meaning of Masonry and proves its claim to be acknowledged as the benefactor of mankind—born in the very cradle of the race. Fellowcrafts are encouraged to study the meanings flowing from those antique symbols and to learn much more. The streams of learning that flow full and broad must be followed to their heads in the springs of the remote past. The history of man's ascent, the origin and evolution of his religions and the wisdom imparted by his ever developing philosophy announces a truth also essential to a free society: "God is above all and the Father of all; in the presence of His infinity, human distinctions are infinitely insignificant." In short, Fellowcrafts are expected to eventually understand, in the heart as well as in the mind, that men best prosper when they live as a brotherhood of man under the Fatherhood of God.

The origin of the ceremonies used during the conferral of the Second Degree of Freemasonry is not precisely known. Some attribute them to Sir Francis Bacon, others to Sir Isaac Newton, both of whom were members of the Royal Society in England, which promoted the sophisticated pursuit of science and the liberal arts. If true, there is little wonder that during that ceremony a candidate's attention is directed to architecture, geometry, astronomy and other arts and sciences. In each discipline, one learns about symmetry, order, consistency and the impact of the heavens upon the earth. The latter, viewed from a Hermetic perspective, also invites the candidate to understand the phrase, "as it is above, so shall it be below."

WITHIN THE LENGTH
OF MY CABLETOW

"I draw them with the cords of a
man, with bands of love…"
Hos. 11:4

Freemasons are, by nature, generally possessed of boundless good intentions. But, each of us is limited by our own capacities and the time we have available to us. Our commitments to church, family, work, and the community in which we live restricts what each of us may give to our Ancient Craft. Consequently, because all our other endeavors are equally important, Masons should be vigilant against overextending themselves; promising more than each can deliver; and delivering less than our best. Such, in and of itself, has the potential to marginalize the Mason who so errs bringing down upon him discredit to his well-earned good reputation and scorn to the covenant of fraternity.

The cable tow is used symbolically in Freemasonry to express that fraternal covenant, which is also emblematic of the great covenant God made with Abraham to honor his descendants. God expected no less from man, who is expected to fear God and obey His commandments. Similarly, Freemasonry requires obedience from its members in giving of oneself to duty, work, devotion and honor. Yet, much like many of Abraham's rude and disobedient descendants, who promised a greater devotion to God than they were prepared to actually give, Masons who commit to act then disappear when the time to act arrives place themselves in jeopardy of being regarded as unreliable.

The phrase "a cable's length" serves as a reminder to every Freemason that there are times when it is much wiser to answer "no" when asked to engage in an activity. When time or other commitments do not prudently allow for the inclusion of more tasks, a Mason's "yes" is evidence of an exercise of poor judgment. Or, it is a signal of insecurity in the love and affection of a Mason's Masonic brethren. Neither is a virtue contained within any Masonic lesson.

Strictly a phrase found only in Freemasonry, "a cable's length" has been given the literal meaning of three miles in length, or the maximum distance required of an Entered Apprentice in attending his Lodge. In a more general sense, the phrase is emblematic of the scope of man's reasonable ability to perform any task. Therefore, we are expected to learn from it that we should carefully weigh that which we propose to undertake before doing so.

Just as Jesus taught the disciples to look inward unto themselves, we, too, can learn much about our own limitations by taking the time necessary to internally reflect upon the scope of our personal abilities. When an hour is available, one cannot very well promise two. If one is of meager economic means, it is not reasonable to expect a life devoted to philanthropy. Unskilled hands can hardly be expected to build a Temple without help from more skilled laborers. The failure of one Mason to discover his own limitations deprives the whole society of the brotherly labors that he is able to undertake.

No Mason ever has, or ever will be expected to act beyond the length of his cable tow. The covenant that binds us to the fraternity does not require us to forego church, family, the community, or our employment. It simply asks us to commit to what we can do based upon the scope of our reasonable abilities. When we so act, harmony is the result, not personal recrimination. Integrity, too, is served, because Masons are being honest about what they can give of themselves. Brotherhood is increased, because vows are not broken.

When a Mason's Lodge asks him to make a commitment, it also asks him to weigh well what it is he is willing to promise and to recall that once the promise is made, a Mason's word is sacred.

A TEST OF FAITH

"But without faith it is impossible to please him:
for he that cometh to God must believe that He is,
and that He is a rewarder of them that diligently seek Him."
Heb. 11:6

In the horrible aftermath of the 9/11/01 Attack on America we were tempted to ask, "Where was God during one of our darkest hours?" Did the Supreme Architect fall asleep when we needed Him? Did he sit idly by while lives were lost and America's way of living changed forever? Is God truly intent upon permitting evil to attack virtue and watch as we suffer?

Those questions, as well as many other similar concerns were asked by Americans across the land as we watched the World Trade Center buckle and slowly crumble to the ground in a cloud of hideous dust. Yet, across this land, Masons also recognized that hour of sorrow as a time of opportunity; a moment in history when the virtues of our Ancient Craft could be practiced for the greater good of all humanity. Those who knew their God well anticipated and believed that He would reveal His power and move to defeat tyranny, terrorism and hatred, just as he had done many times before throughout history.

Freemasonry teaches that faith is the first rung of that theological ladder which Jacob, in his vision, saw reaching from Earth to heaven. It is the cement that holds the ladder together as we climb higher toward the celestial "lodge" above. Faith and trust in our God is an essential requirement for membership in our Order. Both are emphasized in every ritual degree and each stands tall as pillars of true character. As Masons, we are also taught that the Supreme Architect does not sit passively as good people are attacked, maimed and killed by angry, hateful men. Working within those who have faith, He calls the willing soul to labor and motivates that soul to chase away the darkness with intense light.

It is said that out of every act of evil, a good act follows as surely as day follows the night. Those good acts do not simply occur miraculously; they spring from a faithful breast, emblematically represented in Freemasonry by the steadfast keeping of vows and a sincere practice of the virtues revealed in Masonic symbols and ritual. The hour of opportunity at hand when evil arrives asks all men, but particularly Masons to rise above vengeance and practice justice; to apply compassion, not hatred; and to search our hearts for answers about how we can best do unto our neighbor what it is that we should that he would do unto us.

One may fairly ask, "How do we know whether or not we are faithful to God?" The profound reply is when we have freely submitted our own will to His power. Acts of high provocation require equally high acts of virtue, if man is to rise above the endless tit-for-tat inherent in the mentality of hate. When terrorists strike and spew violence across the scene, it is insufficient to simply reply with overwhelming repelling force. Of course men should defend themselves when evil approaches, but man should also see such situations as opportunities to practice eliminating the darkness with the light; of seeking to apply good in place of bad; and, of replacing evil with acts of genuine kindness. The lesson we are continuously learning is that we are all brothers and children of God; those who practice good deeds, as well as those who practice evil. We hate the evil in our brother, but we do not hate our brother, for we have all been created in God's image—not just some of us.

True faith is neither blind, nor founded upon false teachings. It cannot be perverted into misapplying wrong for right, but shines forth intently as the strongest light exposing tyranny and hate as the very antithesis of freedom and love. While history has certainly taught us that every man is capable of permitting the seeds of hatred to grow to consuming heights, Freemasonry teaches men to circumscribe their desires and to keep their passions within due bounds toward all mankind—not just toward those whom we like.

Today, perhaps as never before, Freemasonry is very much needed in our world, not simply for its unique ritual and manner of educating the soul, but for its practical principles of faith, hope and charity. Masons everywhere plant seeds of goodness on a daily basis and seek to be supportive of others as another "self." The virtue of regarding our brother as a true equal, when practiced on a widespread scale, is that all absorbing light that can forever chase away the darkness. And it can only be practiced when we sincerely believe that we are all inhabitants of the same planet who are here to aid, support and protect one another under the Divine grace of our Supreme Architect of the Universe.

WHY ARE MASONS REFERRED TO AS *FREEMASONS*?

"A man that hath friends must shew
himself friendly: and there is no friend
that sticketh closer than a brother."
Prov. 18:24

Masonic tradition explains that neither a slave, nor one born in slavery can be admitted into the rites and privileges of the ancient and honorable fraternity of Freemasonry. While this maxim might, at first glance, appear harsh and elitist, it derived from sound logic: one legally bound to another cannot voluntarily assume the oaths and solemn covenants demanded by the "Order." Yet, logical maxims may not precisely account for why the word *Free*mason is used. In fact, some believe that it may have derived more from notions of brotherhood than from conditions of bondage.

The obligation of a distinct affection for fellow members is a characteristic common to many organized societies of men, especially of Masons. Unlike the hitchhiker, who sticks out his thumb and only promises to ride along if you provide the vehicle and the gas, Masons are committed to sharing in the highs and lows experienced during a journey with a "brother." That commitment was never more apparent than during the Middle Ages when our Masonic ancestors were pursued like criminals by kings and prelates, who intended capture, torture, murder and the annihilation of our "Order."

That horror was not inflicted upon vagrants, liars and cheats, but was practiced upon members of an organization that once constituted a Holy Order of the Roman Catholic Church. These were not men deserving of even the mildest punishment, let alone horrendous torture, but Holy Warriors, who suffered the stress and confusion of the sudden betrayal by the their very benefactors. To escape such treachery, our ancestral brethren may have determined to rely only upon the faithfulness of true and trusty friends. Oaths and signs were likely implemented to distinguish friend from foe. Multiple places of lodging would have had to have been arranged to provide rest, shelter and food for friends and brothers on the run. In that circumstance, there would not have been time to quarrel about religious differences, or preferences: lives were in the balance. Survival had to have been paramount. In such a plight, only God could possibly know the outcome.

We know that our French speaking ancestors, who necessarily fled from France following King Philip's treacherous raids upon the Templar priories, landed among other places in England and Scotland bringing with them their rich language, which was often Anglicized by true and trusty English friends. One such French word, "frere," means "brother" when translated into English. It is recorded that both the hunted and their friends in England were referred to by the French Masons as "Frere Masons," or "brother Masons." Although it can never be known for certain, it is very possible that the French phrase was subsequently Anglicized to "Freemason."

What is known for certain is that while experiencing the horrors of treachery, brotherly love, relief and truth not merely survived—it thrived. The present day scourges of loneliness, illness, poverty, prejudice and injustice hunt down our brethren almost as fervently as did the treacherous kings and prelates who hunted our ancestral brothers centuries ago. Masons and their families who suffer such calamities in their daily lives can rely upon the faithfulness of "Frere Masons" for needed comfort and support. Masonic hospitals, homes and financial endowments sustain those brethren and their families who are in need and ask nothing in return. Our Shrine Hospitals have no accounting departments. The health care is free. Our Masonic Homes do not require payment from the destitute Masons. Shelter is willingly provided through the kind contributions of the brethren. Repayment of financial aid is not expected. It is what faithful brethren do when they are needed.

Today, Masons across our nation are fortunate, indeed, to live in a diverse world where disparate customs, ideas and traditions have spawned a growing sense of community, which in turn teaches the truth of the unity of humanity. Regardless of race, creed, sex, age, or religion we are all God's children. Masonry draws the diverse near and causes true friendship to exist among those who might otherwise have remained at a perpetual distance. We are, indeed, *Freremasons.*

THE HOLY SAINTS JOHN

"And thou, child, shalt be called
prophet of the Highest: for thou shalt
go before the face of the Lord to prepare His ways."
Luke 1:76

Every Mason, from the youngest Entered Apprentice to the more enlightened Master Mason, knows that Masonic Lodges are erected to God and dedicated to the Holy Saints John. For years, writers of Freemasonry have struggled to precisely explain why it is that St. John the Baptist and St. John the Evangelist were selected as the patrons of Masonry rather than any one of hundreds of other saints. For example, St. Thomas has always been regarded as the patron saint of architecture, the five orders of which (Tuscan, Doric, Ionic, Corinthian and Composite) are studied extensively by Masons.

Each year, Masonry celebrates an annual feast for each Holy Saint John: June 24 is dedicated to St. John the Baptist, while December 27 is reserved for St. John the Evangelist. Both dates correspond with the summer solstice, on the one hand, and the winter solstice on the other hand. In the summer, the Sun is at its highest apex on June 24th and at its lowest on December 27th from which point it begins again its ascent. This astronomy was held in very sacred regard by many of the Ancients, who saw the celestial heavens as symbolic of Divine Influence. God's light shone brightest at the summer solstice and weakest on the winter solstice.

As related to us in Holy Scripture, John the Baptist was the son of a High Priest who ministered inside the temple in Jerusalem referred to as Herod's Temple, built by the Jews to replace the destroyed Temple of Solomon. Only the most sacred from the lineage of Zadok were permitted entry into the Sanctum Santorum. The masses conducted their worship outside. John consumed neither wine nor strong drink, wore only hair-cloth and leather, preached repentance by a watery baptism, and taught charity, liberality, justice and fair dealing. Born a Pharisaic Jew, he nevertheless denounced both the Pharisees and Saduccees as vipers, loathing their respective but distinct emphasis on ritualistic religiosity. Though his followers traveled a path of exclusion after his death, refusing to admit anyone within their circle who did not eat the foods they ate, or adhere to the rules they adopted, John traveled a much different path. Believing that all men were of God's kingdom and that virtue was more important than ritual, John zealously led those who would follow his example to search for God's kingdom within man's soul and live life praising God and serving all men as brothers.

By deed and example, John the Baptist opened the door that led to greater enlightenment and, according to Gnostic Christian thought, presided over the baptism of Jesus at the very moment his own divine nature was revealed by God. Throughout his lifetime, John had predicted that occasion, never knowing whether it would be he, or someone else, such as Jesus, who would be "anointed." John's greatest character trait was a devout willingness to serve and sow even though he might not reap all that he had sown during his lifetime. He encouraged even his own followers to seek the source, the truly Divine and conform their lives to the truth emanating from its Light.

Where John the Baptist led mankind to the door that would open hearts and souls to greater understanding, John the Evangelist opened the door that allowed us to enter and walk around the room. His apocalyptic work Revelations, set forth as the last book of the New Testament in the Holy Bible, subtly disclosed to the discerning reader that just as the Kingdom of Heaven is within us, the apocalyptic events described were intended for us to look beyond the events themselves and behold a deeper understanding about creation itself. Both the Hebrew Kabbalah and Gnostic Christianity teach that owing to his free will, man can choose to be Divine, or to embrace sin. The choices he makes impact the continuum of creation, the ongoing cause and effect of life, and can either lead to the joyful union of spirit and nature, or to utter destruction.

The teachings of John the Evangelist demonstrate great energy and poetic fire. His essential lesson to us is that virtue is its own reward, a concept embraced by Freemasons around the world. He spoke of God and man's relation to Him, not of doctrine. He seized upon the imagery in the Book of Ezekiel of a God symbolized in part by fire, or zeal for all that is holy, not upon which ritual man should select to become holy. And, he believed that man could scale the heights and ascend to his Divine destiny, rather than succumb to the enslaving bonds of a meaningless outward and rigid religiosity.

While writers will likely continue to debate why the Holy Saints John were selected as the patrons of Freemasonry, and further enlighten us in the process, Masons everywhere will continue to practice the virtues and pursue the truths taught us by these devout men of God. Look within yourself when you think of John the Baptist and discover your Divinity. When your eyes behold nature, ask the spirit within you to draw you closer to the sounds, the smells and the beauty God has created and resolve to aid Him in His continuing creation.

THE MASTER'S HAT

"The rich and the poor meet together:
the Lord is the maker of them all."
Prov. 22:2

Masonic writers have offered scant insight into the tradition behind the top hat worn by every Worshipful Master of a Masonic Blue Lodge. Indeed, little information is available from which to identify the date, precise or approximate, the custom was adopted. Ancient history reveals that among the Romans, "the hat" was considered a sign of freedom.

In times past, all Masons wore hats while in lodge as a symbol of both freedom and brotherly equality. In the English and American lodges of today, "the hat" is exclusively an attribute of the Worshipful Master's costume. For a better understanding about the meaning of this custom and symbol, it is helpful to examine each object of the symbolism of "the hat" more closely.

The freedom that so clearly distinguishes Freemasonry from all other fraternal organizations is "freedom of faith," which is predominant in Masonic literature. The right of each man to worship the Supreme Architect of the Universe in the manner his heart best loves exemplifies the spirit of the Craft. Until recent times, religious freedom was unknown throughout the world except by those who defied the law of the land in which they lived and endured persecution.

Prior to the American Revolution it was against the law in most of the colonies not to go to church. Not just any church, but to the church selected by the government for each respective colony. Quakers, Baptists, Congregationalists, Presbyterians, Catholics and Jews were held to be criminals in those colonies where that specific religion was not government approved. Fortunately for posterity, our Nation's Founding Fathers adopted and implemented principles of Freemasonry to abolish state sponsored religion. The separation of church and state was, for the first time in world history, instituted as the basis upon which religious tolerance and freedom of faith was founded.

Brotherly equality, so often symbolized in Masonic lodges by the implement known as the "level," teaches us that mankind is the offspring of God; that all men are created by God of one blood with certain inalienable rights to life, liberty and the pursuit of happiness. This truly Masonic metaphysical concept, adopted by the Founding Fathers in the country's Constitution, recognizes that although each one of us possesses different gifts, we are all subject to the same infirmities, the same divine love, the same death and the same final judgment. As such, Freemasons are bound to act equitably with all human distinctions and preserve those inalienable rights for all generations.

The title "Worshipful Master," or "Master of the Lodge," far from denoting lordship, implies that the person so presiding is both a teacher of Masonic symbolism and a director of Masonic conduct. As such, he is required to lead in the interpretation and implementation of lessons in Freemasonry, the most prominent of which, again symbolized by "the hat," are freedom of faith and brotherly equality. When Masons observe the hat tipped in lodge by the Worshipful Master during ritual, they are reminded that it is the Supreme Architect of the Universe to whom they are thankful; in His name that they are influenced to respect and tolerate the rights of all humanity; and, by whose power they are to extend equality and justice in both thought and deed to every man, woman and child.

THE ENTERED APPRENTICE APRON

"Your lamb shall be without blemish…!"
Ex. 12:5

Worn by the initiate in Freemasonry with the flap turned up, the apron of the Entered Apprentice represents the *Cubical Stone* surmounted by the *Pyramid.* Its triangular flap is one face of the *Pyramid* and the whole is a square surmounted by a triangle. If this apron is given to the initiate without further explanation about the true symbolism, it will remain forever very confusing.

The pure white color of the apron represents what is known as "essential light," or as the Ancients declared, the Deity Himself. The lambskin material from which the apron is fashioned symbolizes the *Paschal Lamb*, which according to Mosaic law was the most acceptable offering any man could make to God. It is held equally sacred by Christian Masons, because the white lambskin apron also symbolizes *the Lamb of God that taketh away the sins of the world.* No Freemason is considered fully "clothed," as that term is used to describe a Mason sitting in a tiled lodge, if he wears an apron of any color other than white made of any material other than lambskin. The various ornamental aprons simply do not represent "essential light."

The Masonic legend explained during the Entered Apprentice Degree adds a veil that conceals yet a deeper meaning about the upturned flap itself. During the ritual, the initiate is informed that the upturned flap was originally intended to protect certain Temple workmen from having their clothing soiled. The actual esoteric meaning is, as follows: (1) the Entered Apprentice in King Solomon's Temple worked in the Northeast Corner upon what was known as *the rough ashlar,* a rude and imperfect stone cut from rock quarries; (2) the Fellowcraft toiled in the Southeast Corner of the Temple (where Masonic cornerstones were anciently laid, and indeed still should be laid to be absolutely accurate with the past construction methods employed by our Masonic ancestors) upon the *simple cube,* or *perfect ashlar* (a smoothed *rough ashlar*) that has six faces that are perfect squares; (3) to the Master Mason alone belongs the *pointed cubical,* or square, because shaped as a *Pyramid* it represents spirituality, intellect and Divine intuition; and (4) the upturned flap is also symbolic of the mute and unexplained promise, similar to that of the *square and compasses* situated upon the altar, that if the Entered Apprentice works well and his master is content with his progress, he will in due time attain to an even higher and more perfect *light.*

When a new Masonic initiate is welcomed into a lodge, each Master Mason has an obligation to share in nurturing his progress in Freemasonry. If he is left to his own devices, it is impossible for him to learn that which is only possessed by a Freemason who has devoted time to thorough study about the Craft. If the initiate does not learn, he either leaves the fraternity, or becomes useless to the advancement of its spiritual purpose. Should he leave, where would he possibly travel to obtain the same *light* Freemasonry shines? In truth, there is nowhere for him to go. He loses Freemasonry and Freemasonry loses him. Therefore, the important duty to convey Masonic knowledge must never go ignored.

"Essential light" is creative, abundant, kind, loving and very giving. It needs no man to accomplish its purpose, because it is of God, about God and radiates from God. However, it will use, as God will use, the willing body, the working mind and the devoted spirit to spread abundant love. For ages, Freemasonry has constituted such a willing body of men and shall likely do so until the end of time, as long as Freemasons remain interested and dedicated to learning and imparting the wisdom and truth it has acquired from time immemorial.

THE WINDING STAIRCASE

"Therefore thou shalt keep the Commandments
of the Lord thy God to walk in His ways
and to fear Him."
Deut. 8:6

Commencing at the porch of King Solomon's Temple there was an impressive series of winding steps leading up to the middle chamber of that stupendous edifice. According to the teachings of Freemasonry, there were fifteen such steps, which are significantly explained to the candidate for degrees during the Fellowcraft Degree. The extraordinary symbolism associated with those steps constitutes the basis for acknowledging the close relationship of Freemasonry to Hermetic philosophy and related religious thinking.

To every Freemason, King Solomon's Temple symbolizes a world purified by Shekinah, or the Divine presence in its feminine form, i.e. wisdom. During the Entered Apprentice Degree, the initiate passes from darkness and begins a journey through the mysteries of the Temple, which is nothing greater than witnessing the truths of the world in God's presence. The mere fact that the steps are winding further symbolizes a world consisting of a spiral, as opposed to a closed circle, representing the avenue God uses to communicate with His creation.

In the Fellowcraft Degree, the candidate makes further progress in his search for light, which is the wisdom of God, by first passing through two pillars of strength and establishment. Strength is related to King David with whom God made a special covenant to use David's ancestral line from which to deliver the Messiah, thereby "establishing" the House of David as divine. The candidate then begins the laborious climb upward, step-by-step toward the goal, which is nothing less than possessing the *Word*, or Divine truth.

Continuous self improvement is acknowledged as a solemn duty of every Fellowcraft Mason; perfection is the end sought, which can only be found at the top of the fifteen steps. Those fifteen steps are separated into a series of three, five and seven steps indicating an individual Mason's adaptation to the upward course according to each individual's "strength." At the various pauses in the progression upward special instructions are given the Fellowcraft, which are intended to aid him in his ascent and which can only be attained through a rigid course of self discipline, the cultivation of noble virtues and the fervent practice of righteousness. Intellectual growth, a knowledge of the sciences which contribute to the progress of mankind and the actual attainment of true wisdom are urged by the various symbolic explanations provided the candidate during his ascension.

The seven liberal arts and sciences represent the completion of human learning. The ultimate quest for Divine knowledge beckons the candidate to climb even farther; to recognize the existence of an intellect that transcends the limited intellect of man. The true understanding is achieved when the candidate learns that the transcendent intellect is not separate from himself, but becomes a part of his being when pursued with *faith*. The sublime lesson here is that perfect knowledge of the *true Word* cannot be entirely achieved in this lifetime. Only a "substitute" will be attained. Life beyond illuminated *truth* is given by God as our reward so that we may continue to learn, work and love.

TWO PERPENDICULAR PARALLEL LINES

"See then that ye walk circumspectly,
not as fools, but as wise."
Eph. 5:15

During the lecture in the Entered Apprentice degree, the candidate's attention is eventually directed to a point within a circle, which is supported by two perpendicular parallel lines. The point is intended to represent an individual brother and the circle the boundary line of his conduct. The two perpendicular parallel lines represent Saint John the Baptist and Saint John the Evangelist, whom the candidate is informed were imminent patrons of Freemasonry. At a deeper level, this combination of Masonic symbols invites meditation upon the importance of living a circumspect life and precisely how such a life is in complete harmony with God and the universe.

In order that one may better understand the original source of this special imagery, it is essential to study the various ancient mysteries observed by the Chinese and Japanese. Those mysteries were founded on the same principles as the mysteries that originated in India and, indeed, were expressed by very similar rites. Among the many symbols used in those rites was a ring supported by two serpents, emblematic of a world protected by the power and wisdom of the great Creator. In time, those two serpents gave way to the current Masonic symbolism of two perpendicular parallel lines, which support the circle. Those lines are termed "perpendicular," because each forms a right angle with the circle signifying the unification of different lessons in philosophy and religion.

By the circle, we are reminded that as man walks circumspectly through life, cautious in his choice of words and deeds, he walks as God intended and in full accord with His laws. The parallel lines also remind us of the several characteristics of the Holy Saints John: a steady reproval of vice on the one hand, and a faithful effort at discharging our duties to God, including the cultivation of brotherly love among all men. The perpendicular configuration of those lines further reminds us that morality, duty and charity are tools speculative Masons use to erect their spiritual building, that house not made with hands, eternal in the heavens.

Freemasonry consistently teaches about the relationship of light to darkness, goodness to evil. God is light and in Him there is no darkness at all. Yet, whence came the darkness and why does it run parallel in our lives to light? Who permitted evil to travel a path perpendicular to good? What part does man's free will actually play in these things?

Freemasonry beckons us to struggle against the animal instincts of immorality, selfishness and contempt of others. Instead, Masons are prompted to follow the example of the Holy Saints John and in so doing to live as the Creator so intended man to live. Human beings are suppose to love life as God loves it—He would not have created that which he hated. We are expected to find joy in the performance of duty to others, just as God rejoices in pouring out His blessings upon mankind. For these, and the many other blessings, Freemasons should constantly bow their heads and softly utter a prayer of thanksgiving and high praise for all that afflicts us, as well as for all that benefits us.

Affliction and beneficence are yet another example of parallels running throughout mankind's earthly existence. Man is not always benefited by what he encounters, neither is he always afflicted. During an entire lifetime, the good most often balances out the bad.

It is our endurance of the one and joyful basking in the other that builds our character, instills within us that sense of duty to others and overwhelms us with a true sense of brotherly love and affection for our neighbors.

THE CABLE-TOW

"I drew them with cords of a man,
with bands of love..."
Hos. 11:4

Several Masonic writers, including Albert Pike, see no meaning in the cable-tow beyond the fact that it is used either to lead an initiate into the lodge room, or pull him outside in the event he proves unworthy. However, applying such a non-symbolic interpretation is highly unusual in Freemasonry. The entirety of a Masonic lodge is a symbol, as is every object and act, which fit together revealing truths to such eyes and ears that are prepared to see and hear.

The obligations assumed and vows taken by candidates are literally ties that bind each Mason to the fraternity. When those obligations are broken, or the vows ignored, the offending member is excused possibly never again to return. In and of itself, that fact lends meaning to the cable-tow.

From ancient history and the Holy Bible we learn that the cable-tow is the outward visible symbol of the commitment made to exercise brotherly love, relieve the distressed and always favor the truth. Its length, as well as its strength is measured by the ability each Freemason has to fulfill his obligations. As such, the cable-tow represents both a man's capacity and his character. Just as the umbilical cord is replaced by a tie of love and obligation between mother and child when severed, a candidate is bound to Freemasonry by a tie stronger than his cable-tow as soon as he completes

139

confirming his oaths at the altar. Force is replaced by brotherly love as soon as the cable-tow is removed constituting a Masonic "secret" of safety and security. Freemasons in good standing need never again want for a roof over their head, or food on the table. It will always be provided.

But, let us not too quickly forget that a cable-tow has two ends. One binds a Freemason to the fraternity, the other binds the fraternity to the Freemason. Each obligation is of equal importance; that of the whole to the one, and of the one to the whole. The fraternity is under vows to its members to guide, instruct and train them for the effective service to the Craft, as well as all of humanity. Control, obedience, direction and guidance—these are also meanings attached to the cable-tow.

By control, Freemasonry does not mean to imply that force is involved. To the contrary, Freemasonry "rules" men as beauty rules an artist, or as love rules a lover. Freemasonry "controls" and shapes us through its human touch and moral nobility. By the same power, Freemasonry wins obedience and lends direction and guidance to our lives. At the altar, Freemasons assume vows to follow and obey Freemasonry's highest principles and ideals. Those vows are not empty promises—they are commitments undertaken upon sacred honor.

For each Mason, the cable-tow extends as far as the individual's moral principles and material conditions will allow. Of that distance, each Mason must be the sole and exclusive judge of how much he can give in the way of service to others. When the cable-tow of an individual Mason is joined with those of other Masons, a bond of brotherhood so immense is formed that no mortal can accurately measure.

Brotherhood is, indeed, one of the holiest assets of humanity. There exists an invisible cord binding together every man, woman and child. It winds its way through every human life and draws together the most disparate beliefs making friends of those who might otherwise have remained at a perpetual distance.

THE CORNERSTONE

"The stone which the builders refused is
become the head stone of the corner."
Ps. 118:22-23

In construction, the cornerstone is placed in the corner of two walls in a building. In operative Masonry it is considered the most important stone in the entire edifice. In Masonic buildings, it is required that this stone be situated in the northeast corner of the structure.

In ancient times, the laying of cornerstones of important edifices was completed during very impressive and elaborate ceremonies. Amidst solemn prayers and acts of consecration, dignitaries acted in concert to lay the ponderous stone in its resting place. The speculative Masonic symbolism associated with the cornerstone is no less impressive.

In form, the cornerstone must be perfectly square on its surfaces and its solid contents must form a cube. In Freemasonry, the square is a symbol of morality, while the cube symbolizes truth. The situation of the cornerstone in the northeast also conforms to an even deeper spiritual significance.

To Masons, the north has always been presumed a place of darkness. The east has consistently represented light. Therefore, the progression from north to east symbolizes a Freemason's progress from darkness to light, as he becomes more educated in the workings of the Craft.

The permanence and durable quality of the cornerstone, which is intended to last longer than the edifice itself, reminds us that while the earthly tabernacle we refer to as the human body shall one day pass away, the soul, or cornerstone of immortality, shall never, never, never die. In the Christian religion, that is also symbolized in the person of Jesus. In other religions, it is symbolized simply by the spiritual concept of Deity. In truth, both attach the same meaning and provoke the same understanding about the truth of the soul's eternal existence.

The proper setting of the cornerstone by the implements of operative Masonry—the square, the level and the plumb—further reminds us that our virtues are daily tested by temptation, trial, suffering and adversity. Freemasonry teaches that men must be so tried in order that they may one day be declared true and trusty by the Master Builder. It is then that a Mason achieves the status of being a living stone for that house not made with hands, eternal in the heavens.

After it is set into place, the cornerstone to a Masonic Building is then symbolically set apart from the structure that is to follow by pouring upon its surface corn, wine and oil. As Freemasons are instructed during the Fellowcraft Degree, those three "wages of a Fellowcraft" are emblematic of the nourishment, refreshment and joy, which are to become the rewards of a faithful performance of duty.

The proper reflection upon the lessons taught by the cornerstone reveals that taken together as a whole, they embody all that is taught in Freemasonry. From a firm foundation erected upon a prayerful life, sacrifice and the exercise of brotherly love, Masons who use the tools of the Craft lead better lives and do better work than those unskilled in Freemasonry's workings. The Mason who so acts during his earthly existence is assured of hearing words of Divine approval: "well done my true and faithful servant!" To no loftier goal need any man aspire.

NETWORK, LILY-WORK
AND POMEGRANATES

"A good tree cannot bring forth evil fruit, neither
can a corrupt tree bring forth good fruit."
Matt. 7:18

In the second degree of Freemasonry, the candidate is instructed about the symbolic importance of "network, lily-work and pomegranates." The "network," from the intricate connection of its several parts denotes unity. The "lily-work," from its purity and retired situation of its growth, denotes peace. And, the "pomegranates" from the exuberance of their seeds, denote plenty. These symbols are explained in Masonic instruction as a unit and consequently should be understood as a whole.

Masons are taught that each person has an invisible self, a spirit or soul that constitutes the true essence of man. When the body falls away and the dust returns to the earth, the spirit or soul continues. This was the central instruction given to the special elect in the Ancient Egyptian mysteries and is a truth about the God-like nature of all men that far too few know about, or accept. For that reason, as well as others, the Ancient Egyptians guarded this truth as a secret, or as a pearl that is not to be thrown before swine. A man had to prove himself worthy of receiving such instruction before he was permitted to participate in the ritual.

Like the Ancient Egyptian schooled in the mysteries, Freemasons have a responsibility, while walking through this vale of tears, to nurture the spirit, to look within and try to comprehend the enormous power and innate goodness that dwells deep within each person's consciousness. The combined symbols emblematic of unity, peace and plenty focuses our attention upon the fruits of such nurturing in such a way that we are each enabled to assess our own spiritual growth.

By unity, Freemasonry refers to fraternal love, to the notion that all men are created equal, and to the need to preserve institutions which foster the brotherhood of man. Additionally, the "network" teaches us that when we look at that which is within, we know that the same innate goodness; the same spirit; and the same God dwells within each one of us. Thus, we come to see our brother as another self, not as another person. From this knowledge springs forth in full bloom the beauty of the Golden Rule—a rule that is so very easy for a Mason to follow: "do unto your neighbor that which you would that he should do unto you."

By use of the word "peace," one most often thinks about the physical condition of the world. When our nations and countries are not at war slaughtering innocent beings we are said to be at "peace." Yet, the "lily-work" actually symbolizes something other than world peace. It teaches us that within our inner being where our "secret center" hosts the Great Architect of the Universe, a powerful peace is available to us. Man's intellect instructs his outward behavior and is regarded as the seat of the soul. Intellect allows man to be fearful, to act cowardly, to behave bravely and even to select love above hatred. When one chooses wisely, the peace within not only calms one's mood, it also alters behavior toward others. In that state of mind, one man can truthfully declare to his friend and brother, "my peace I give you."

By considering the concept of plenty, Masons learn to consistently live "on purpose," that is with an attitude of giving service abundantly. The Davidic bloodline from which King Solomon emerged required that family members serve their fellow man. It was considered unworthy to govern for the purpose of controlling others, or to merely perpetuate power over others. Freemasons, too, have the choice to serve, or to live a life of being served by others. The former is Masonic, the latter is something else. Freemasonry does not judge the choice made. However, its symbols teach us that there are natural consequences which follow each choice made. The Holy Bible instructs that from he who has little, much more will be taken away; but to he who has much, to him shall much more be given.

From these three symbols, we also learn that there is no unity without peace and plenty. There is no brotherhood of man without one man giving to another as prompted by the Divine light within him.

THE ASHERAH, OR "RODS"

"And the Lord said unto Moses, 'Put forth thine hand
and take it (serpent) by the tail'. And he put forth
his hand and…it became a rod in his hand."
Ex. 4:4

One Masonic writer stated that the rod of Moses, fearful to the Egyptians as the attack of a serpent, was a scepter of righteousness to the Children of Israel. As the scripture passage above taken from The Book of Exodus implies, the rod was a symbol of Divine authority— a visible demonstration of God's power. In some religions that meaning of the rod morphed. For example, in Christianity the rod denoted a type of Christ's death to which Freemasonry ultimately points; for as by a serpent death came into the world, so by the death of the Son of Man was the serpent and Satan fully vanquished. Another provocative interpretation can be gleaned from a deeper inspection of ancient Masonic history.

A Masonic Temple is intended to be a representation of King Solomon's Temple, which displayed astronomical characteristics similar to those found within an Enochian Temple. Situated due east and west, the eastern end of today's Masonic Temple is where the Worshipful Master sits representing the sunrise at the equinox. At the opposite end, the Senior Warden sits in the west where he represents the sun setting at equinox. The Junior Warden is stationed in the south of the Masonic Temple and represents the moon, beauty, wisdom—the feminine principle.

Several English Masonic Temples display a blazing star with the letter "G" affixed to the center of the ceiling. The blazing star represents the sun, around which is a five-pointed star which has scant interpretation among Masonic writers. However, that imagery was exceptionally important to the biblical character Enoch, as well as the so-called "Grooved-Ware People," who were an ancient society of humans who also knew about the importance of the 40-year Venus cycle. Indeed, until the atomic clock was invented, there was no more accurate means of determining time than studying the position of Venus against the backdrop of the stars.

The rods carried by the Stewards and Deacons in a Masonic lodge were originally called "wands." They represented the measuring rods which the Canaanites and early Jews called "Asherah." Asherah was the name of the goddess who was regarded as the mother of the dawn and the dusk, symbolized astronomically by Venus. The purpose of those Asherah was originally to determine the angles of the sunrise and sunset as indicated by the shadows cast from the vertically held staffs. The Deacons were originally essential for orienting the location of the Temple by finding two days a year where the shadow of the rising sun perfectly aligned with the shadow of the setting sun, i.e., the equinoxes.

In the Entered Apprentice degree, the candidate is placed in the northeast corner of the lodge room. A Deacon holds the candidate with one hand, an Ashrah, or rod with the other. In that place, according to Enochian legend, the Deacon and candidate were standing on the summer solstice sunrise line marked by the shadow of the pillar named "Jachin." In the second degree in many Masonic lodges, the candidate is placed in the southeast corner on the winter solstice sunrise line denoted by the shadow from the pillar called "Boaz." In the third degree, some lodges place the candidate on the center line representing the perfect east-west line of the equinoxes.

During the era of the original Knights Templar, as well as during the early years of European Freemasonry, the Asherah were put to practical use. In the building of the hundreds of cathedrals, Asherahs were used to measure the angle of the sun's first shadow when laying the foundation stone, or "cornerstone." That resulted in the cathedrals facing the rising sun on one of two specific days of the year—the summer solstice, or the winter solstice.

Thus, the rods carried in the Masonic lodges of today represent symbols of man's effort to measure the universe. Although each rod bears an image of the sun or moon, their significance in today's Masonic ritual is forgotten. But, to the Freemason who studies such things, those rods serve as reminders of the great emphasis Freemasonry places upon the study of science, geometry and astronomy.

SEVEN:
THE SACRED NUMBER

"And he had in his right hand seven stars..."
Rev. 1:16

In every religious system of antiquity, particularly in the Ancient Egyptian mysteries, the number seven held a place of veneration. The Hebrew term for seven suggests sufficiency, or fullness, thereby signifying perfection. The great candlestick at King Solomon's Temple consisted of seven holders which were symbolically derived from the ancient studies of the planets, and represented the seven presiding archangels. Christians also regard seven as sacred and believe that the seven stars mentioned in the scripture passage above taken from The Book of Revelation represent the seven true messengers of Christ. The number seven is no less revered and venerated by Masonic symbolism.

Ancient intellect attributed numbers to the creative genius of God. Mathematics was seen as the revelation of principles associated exclusively with the Divine mind. Saint Augustine and Martin Luther both taught that the number seven must be considered sacred, because of its repetition in scripture. As an example, the Holy Bible states that Jacob served Rachel's father for seven years; there were seven years of plenty and seven years of famine when Joseph governed Egypt; Samson was bound with seven bands; and, on the seventh day when seven priests blew seven trumpets while circling the walls of Jericho seven times, the walls collapsed and the town fell to Joshua.

Our first Most Excellent Grand Master, Solomon, King of Israel, lectured upon the seven pillars of wisdom and taught that the number seven represented Infinite Wisdom in relationship to Infinite Power. Drawing upon those teachings, Freemasonry has adopted the philosophy that while the occurrence of such wisdom and power logically suggests that one who has the power to do good work also possesses the power to work even greater evil. Only in the hands of God are the two held in equilibrium resulting in infinite harmony throughout the universe.

Yet, humans are incapable of living harmoniously by doing both good and evil. One destroys the other. Darkness gives way to light. A lighted lamp brought into a darkened room chases away the darkness. The two cannot reside side-by-side. Freemasons are asked to understand what it means to live in the light, to understand human limitations and to promptly replace perceived cruelties with abundant acts of kindness.

Man is imperfect. The perfect number seven is but a goal that is quite possibly unattainable during this earthly existence. Within mankind's limitations, falsehoods can never become truth. Intolerance cannot beget compassion. Murder does not return men to life. Such powers reside exclusively with God. Therefore, the number seven teaches us that because perfection eludes us, Freemasons should strive to work acts of charity, to circumscribe their desires and to keep their passions within due bounds toward all mankind.

THE NORTH IS TERMED A PLACE OF DARKNESS

"But, the Lord liveth, which brought up
and which led the seed of the house
of Israel out of the north country,..."
Jer. 23:8

Candidates are instructed in the Entered Apprentice Degree that the three lights of Freemasonry are situated in the east, west and south of the lodge room. According to Masonic legend, there is none in the north, because King Solomon's Temple was situated in such a manner that neither the Sun, nor moon, at meridian height, could bring light into the Temple from the north. Therefore, the candidate is informed that among Masons, the north is always termed a place of darkness.

As with other Masonic symbols, this, too, invites meditation upon the questions about light and darkness, good and evil. Here, our contemplation is focused upon a new consideration about these opposites. The candidate is not told that King Solomon's Temple was situated in a particular location to serve as a geography lesson. Rather, he is so informed, because the Holy Writings symbolize the north as the direction from which evil flows.

Should you continue to read further in the Book of Jeremiah, you will curiously learn that the prophet indicated that all matters of wickedness from adultery to the worship of false gods flowed from the north. It is not likely that Jeremiah was being literal with these words. To the contrary, it is quite likely he intended to communicate a very valuable spiritual lesson that is also revealed in The Bahir, one of the oldest, most important, and most carefully preserved of all ancient Kabbalah texts.

The Ineffable Name is said to be pronounced, "Yod, He, Vav, He." According to ancient Hebrew theology, the Name, if understood, conveys the complete meaning of existence and God. Among other esoteric considerations, a thorough study of the Ineffable Name necessarily opens the door to a deep review of the concept of Zer Anpin, which theologically consists of six different directions represented by the "Vav." Far too simply stated, what is meant is that the pursuit of wisdom is closer to the pursuit of God than is the worldly pursuit of establishing kings and kingdoms.

More fundamentally, Zer Anpin represents the essence of the fact that many possible futures arise from man's exercise of free will. We can choose to be hateful, angry, sullen, hostile and unfriendly. In so doing we have also assured ourselves of a very specific future: a life full of spite, revenge and conflict. On the other hand, man can select kindness, compassion, faith, hope and charity as his characteristics. The difference in the future is like the difference between night and day, light and darkness.

Radiance, or the vertical connection to supernal divinity is symbolized in Freemasonry, as well as in most ancient religions, by the Sun, Moon and Mercury (note the similarity between this array and that told the candidate about the Sun, Moon and Master of the Lodge) traveling a path from east to west. Neither of those bodies travels north to south, although during the vernal equinox, the east to west path necessarily touches distinctly upon the southern hemisphere. The spirit of divinity that is thought by many to dwell within every man is said to be strengthened by exposure to the "radiance." Forces associated with the north are said to flow from the material world only and thereby incite worldly desires for such non-spiritual things as fame, wealth and power.

May it always be so that the north is termed a place of darkness among Masons. Freemasonry seeks to instill faith, hope and charity. Masons live compassionate lives. The members of a lodge constitute a brotherhood of man under the fatherhood of God. Freemasonry seeks not to give a man a futile future, one devoid of love, peace and harmony. Wholly to the contrary, the Order seeks to instill this great commandment: love God with all of your heart and soul, and love your neighbor as you love yourself.

THE TROWEL

"Behold, how good and how pleasant it is for
brethren to dwell together in unity."
Ps. 133:1

The trowel is the symbol of that which has the power to bind men together. What is this unifying power? We frequently meet with men who seem to lack unity in their makeup; a spirit of disorganization or anarchy is at work in them so that they seem to live at cross-purposes with themselves. What they know they should do they do not, and many things which they do they do against their own will. They may have personal force, but it is scattered and their lives never come into focus.

Of these men we say that they lack character. Character comes from the word that originally meant a graving tool; after long use the name of the tool came to be applied to the engraving itself, and thus the term has come to stand for a man whose actions give one an impression of definiteness and clear-cuttedness, like an engraving. The trowel is intended to remind us of that true character, the essential ingredient necessary for one man to properly bond with another.

Francis Bacon so thoroughly exemplified the spirit of fraternalism, that is of men bonding together to perform works of great charity, that his memory is largely associated with the Fellowcraft Degree. Bacon was at various times in his life Lord Chancellor of England, a philosopher, an author, a statesman, scientist, orator and humorist.

He was one of the prophets of the scientific revolution and instigated the formation of the Royal Society. Bro. Bacon edited the first King James version of the Holy Bible and is thought by many to actually have authored several works attributed to Shakespeare.

Bacon secretly founded the first Lodge of Free & Accepted Masons in England. He wrote the second degree ritual, which by his creation emphasized the liberal arts and sciences. In addition, he founded the first Rosicrucian Brotherhood and secretly laid the groundwork for the eventual establishment of the United States of America. Using Masonic symbolism, Bacon wrote the *New Atlantis*, which many contend contains the keys to all Masonic ritual.

Bacon's example, so essential to the true symbolism of the Trowel, was that of a Master Mason building for the future. In building for the future, one must instill in others the vital essence of one's own purpose. Bacon's dreams were realizable because the early Freemasons embraced his vision and purpose. His dreams were the cement that bound the brotherhood to the process of regeneration, that is, to everlasting renewal.

That philosophy is embodied in the three degrees of Freemasonry. From grade to grade, the candidate is led from an old to an entirely new quality of life. The candidate begins his Masonic life as the natural man and ends it by becoming a regenerated "perfected" man. He symbolically rises from the dead a Master, a just man made perfect, with larger consciousness and faculties, an efficient instrument for use by the Great Architect in His plan of rebuilding the Temple of fallen humanity, and capable of advancing other men to a participation in the same great work.

Thus, the Trowel also teaches us that the real purpose of modern Freemasonry is, not the social and charitable purposes to which so much appropriate attention is paid, but the expediting of the spiritual evolution of those who aspire to perfect their own nature and transform it into a more god-like quality. The challenge of Freemasonry is to be reborn "incorruptible" which must be preceded by the death of the lower nature. Consequently, the intention of Masonry is not the building of a temple, but the greater science of soul building using the cement of brotherly love and affection.

THE WIDOW'S SON

"He was a widow's son of the
tribe of Naphtali,…"
1 Kings 7:14

It is typically held within Masonic circles that Hiram Abif, the original architect of King Solomon's Temple, was actually the son of a widow of the tribe of Naphtali, who probably married a man of Tyre after the death of Hiram's father. In that Hiram enjoys such a position of imminence in Freemasonry, it is also believed that the natural reverence Masons bestowed upon the memory of his widowed mother was the basis for Freemasonry's later devotion to the support of the widows of all Masons. The earliest recorded Masonic rituals dating back to the late 1600's include passages demanding that all good Masons make a special effort to care for such special women. Yet, as is true of most symbols in Freemasonry, that of the "widow's son" is also very relevant to man's relationship to the Deity.

In Grail lore, certain ancient writers, such as Sir Thomas Malory, explored the connection of Jesus' family to the hereditary line of King David and beyond. The stories that were associated with the rich King Arthur legends were expressed as such to protect "believers" from being accused as heretics and possibly suffering horrible deaths as a result. It is believed that tarot cards originated for the same reason and thus are also a part of the concealed expression of belief that Jesus and his family may be traced to David and Abraham.

Freemasonry's Hiram Abif is also identified in Grail lore as the Son of a Widow, personified in the character known as Percival, one of the Grail champions Malory identified together with Lancelot and Sir Galahad. Percival is also sometimes identified as a grand-nephew of Joseph of Arimathea, whom some believe is none other than Jesus' own brother James. Thus, for Grail adherents, the stories establish nothing less than a bloodline traceable directly to Divinity.

The original Widow of the Grail bloodline was Ruth the Moabite (heroine of the Old Testament Book of Ruth), who married Boaz and was the great-grandmother of King David. Her descendants were called "Sons of the Widow." In this context, Hiram Abif is revealed as a descendant of Ruth, whose ancient forerunners included Tubal-cain, the first artificer in metals. Can this be the purpose for deliberately incorporating the phrase "widow's son" into essential Masonic ritual?

The true Mason is an ardent seeker after knowledge. He knows that Freemasonry has not selected its symbols for idle purposes, but to teach valuable and important lessons about God, brotherhood and charity. The chance selection of the "widow's son" as symbolism is as likely as was the chance selection of the square and compasses. Masons are told very little about Hiram Abif and it is rather odd that such a central person should nowhere appear in the Holy Bible. Some will point to various passages and report they have there found Hiram, but nowhere is there a man named Hiram Abif who is also referred to as the "widow's son."

If we accept the Grail lore interpretation, we also acknowledge that the Grand Master Hiram Abif is as important a character as is King Solomon, whom we also know from Old Testament scripture to be a son of King David. If we reject that interpretation, we are back to square one: what does Freemasonry mean when it alludes to its most central character as a Son of a Widow? Perhaps the phrase is derived from another religious source.

Manicheanism was founded by the Persian sage Mani in approximately 240 AD. His followers believed that the world was divided into kingdoms of light and darkness, good and evil. Those followers, like the descendants of Ruth, were called "sons of the widow," which was an allusion to the Ancient Egyptian Mysteries. In the Osirian mysteries, Isis was widowed when Typhon killed her husband. Typhon was a symbol for darkness and evil, while Isis and her husband were regarded as the female and male principles of light and virtue—the condition God originally intended for His human creatures.

In the New Testament of the Holy Bible, yet another reference to a "widow's son" appears in Luke 7:11-17. There, Jesus has revived the dead son of the Widow of Nain. This woman thereafter proclaimed publicly that in Jesus, God has visited His people.

In his book entitled *The Burning Bush,* Edward Beaugh Smith observed that the phrase "widow's son" appears frequently throughout the Holy Bible, recounts the Manicheanism story and leans strongly upon the Osirian legend as the source of that phrase. Smith's premise relates to what he calls an Evolutionary Epic—a time during which the consciousness will have established in the successors of the "Sons of the Widow" that evil must be overcome by charitableness. Here, Masons at last find the primary lesson intended by this specific symbolism—charity is Masonry's fundamental goal, as fundamental as knowing that our Grand Master Hiram Abif is the "widow's son."

Printed in the United States
59427LVS00002B/65